# REPAIR
# WASHINGTON

*A Practical Resolution to
Call a
Constitutional Convention*

SIDNEY PULITZER
*Businessman, Investor, and
Adjunct Professor of Entrepreneurship
Freeman School of Business*
TULANE UNIVERSITY

ISBN: 149096181X
ISBN 13: 9781490961811

# *Dedication*

*To the Next Generation of Americans*
*May They Live In Freedom*
*And a Land of Opportunity.*

# Acknowledgements

This publication gained immensely because of the efforts of a number of talented people whose counsel and friendship I value most highly. Among these are Tom Grace, attorney and mediator, Timothy Slater, a lifelong friend who suggested a conceptual rewrite; Mike Gretchen, banker and financier; Ira Solomon, Dean of the Freeman School of Business and Angelo DeNisi former Dean of the Freeman School of Business, Tulane University; Professor Douglas Brinkley, historian and author; and Steve Griffin, Professor of Constitutional Law, Tulane University Law School. The support of two special angels Lawrence Kagan and Al Regenbogen is gratefully appreciated. My grateful thanks to Louisiana Representatives Neil Abramson and Nick Larusso who contributed to the completion of the proposed resolution herein.

I am also indebted to Kenneth Marks whose sincere patriotic advice and counsel were invaluable, Janet Bean for her wisdom, and my friend and former secretary Shirley Hill. Thanks also to Michelle Neuschotz Burke who suggested over a decade ago that I write this book. It has taken those many years of research to do the legislation and complete the legislation and amendments.

A special thanks to my son, Sidney Pulitzer Jr., for setting me straight as to what is politically achievable, and what is not. Many grateful thanks to my beautiful wife Joyce Pulitzer. She has been a wonderful and amazing partner for over half a century. Her love, friendship, and loyalty have made my life complete. Without her encouragement this book would never have been written.

# Disclaimer

The contents of this book represent the opinions and views only of the author. It was written with the hope that something good would be forthcoming for our wonderful country.

There may be similarities with other publications, as many of the proposed ideas are already known and popular with the general public. All data and opinions are presented for informational purposes only and are derived from sources believed authoritative and reliable, but not guaranteed.

# Contents

# INTRODUCTION

*"The greatest threat to our Constitution is our own ignorance of it."*

Jacob Roecker

## CALL A CONSTITUTION CONVENTION!

Washington is broken. A 2011 poll reported that 82% of Americans disapproved of Congress and only 8% believed Washington could solve our problems. A 2012 Gallop poll gave Congress a 10% approval rating, the lowest ever. What went wrong? Monumental technological changes have adversely affected how our government functions, and our Constitution has not been kept current. It is time for action.

This book is written to appeal to liberals, conservatives, Democrats and Republicans. It is for all Americans. It explains how to repair the things over two centuries that have gradually gone wrong. Our Founding Fathers knew that over time, evolutionary changes to our central government might require action by the state governments that founded the United States. In our Constitution they wisely provided the legal power for the states to call a Convention, not to write a new Constitution, but to offer prudent Amendments for ratification. We have a national problem that will take a nationwide effort to correct; <u>our Constitution needs updating</u>. Cities rewrite their charters every few decades and states update their constitutions each century. Our Constitution has not been modernized in the 228 years since our nation was founded!

## A CONSTITUTIONAL CONVENTION IS LEGAL

Article V permits two-thirds (34) of our state legislatures to call a Constitutional Convention. Here are the actual words: "... *on the Application of the Legislatures of two-thirds of the several States, shall call a Convention for proposing Amendments, which ... shall be valid to all Intents and Purposes, as Part of this Constitution, when ratified by the Legislatures of three-fourths of the several States,*"

Here are the broad topics covered in this book. If you love our country and want to Repair Washington, this is what we need to do.

1. We need to call a successful Constitution Convention. This legal capability is in our Constitution and requires that 34 states pass a similar resolution to call a convention. That proposed resolution is in the next chapter.
2. This book proposes eleven Amendments. The first three are critical to repairing our election process. They include term limits, election reform, and ethics for public servants. Ratification of all three amendments will dramatically improve the performance of our government.

3. The remaining eight Amendments modernize the limits and powers of our federal and state governments. Their ratification would improve specific areas such as law and order, tort reform, spending discipline, and other important issues.
4. A final chapter addresses the necessity of maintaining a balance between Free Enterprise and Socialism to assure prosperity.

In centuries past Europe had Kings and Queens with all the powers of a dictatorship, and the people had no voice in government. When the United States was established, it was a radical political experiment and continues as a work in progress. Our Founding Fathers decided that all power rested with the people and invented the concept of self-government. "We the People" vote on our leaders and consent to them limited powers sufficient for government to provide protection and other essential services we cannot do for ourselves.

The people consented to grant limited political power to the states. After our first government, the Continental Congress failed, the states sent delegates to the Constitutional Convention to create a viable central government. When the states ratified our Constitution (the voters never voted on it) the states transferred *limited powers* to the United States of America creating our federal government. These powers include national defense, law and order, honest courts, sound money, border control, and more. The system worked well for the first 150 years. Citizen patriots held office for only one or two terms, so half of the Congress changed in each election. But life expectance, technology, population changes and transfers of power have made our federal government dysfunctional.

Today we have professional career politicians who talk beautifully on TV, but serve themselves first, their party second, and our nation last. Professional career politicians are difficult to defeat because our election process is also broken. The technological wonders of TV and the Internet permits hundreds of millions of dollars to win elections, not a candidate's experience, accomplishments, skill or statesmanship. When elections are over the special interests that supplied the advertising money are in control of our nation.

The growth in the population of nine states means that their combined block votes in the Electoral College elect the President. The other 41 states are disenfranchised. My state, Louisiana has no say as to who will be our President, does yours? And our federal government has taken powers to itself not granted by the states or our Constitution. Professional politicians will **never** change this broken system or reduce their power.

**The only way we can Repair Washington is to call a Constitutional Convention to recommend urgently needed Amendments for ratification by the states.**

Calling a Convention will NOT BE EASY and will stir things up in Washington. It will be like kicking over an anthill. There are powerful interests in our Nation's Capital that like things the way they are. Many *special interests* feed at the trough of the trillions in government spending. Wealthy citizens will oppose repeal of legislation that provides them favorable tax treatment and other benefits. Politicians who could no longer run for office if two-term limits were ratified will fight like hell. These wealthy and powerful interests will launch a campaign to try and stop a Convention by misleading and frightening the American People.

They will say we need professional politicians because the government is too complicated, not acknowledging that it is complex because they have made it so. Good Government doesn't have to be complicated, big, or expensive. They will try to frighten us by suggesting that a Constitutional Convention will pass radical Amendments that can make the government dangerously powerful. It already is. They will suggest a Convention will weaken, or limit our freedoms. That too is already happening. There is absolutely no merit to these fear tactics.

Here are the factual reasons that prove a Constitutional Convention is the totally safe and proper way to Repair Washington.

1. Our Founding Fathers created this nation *in a Constitutional Convention*. They lived it and felt it so valuable that they put the right to call another

Convention into our Constitution. Can't we trust their judgment?

2. Each and every amendment must be ratified by no less than three-fourths (38) of the state legislatures. That is so extreme a hurdle that it is more likely good amendments will not be ratified rather than bad ones.

3. The track record of the ratification process is impressively successful. Remember the first ten amendments called "the Bill of Rights?" Well there were twelve amendments, but two couldn't get ten votes from the 13 original states. Bad amendments won't fly. Do you think that 38 state Legislatures that represent liberals, conservatives, Democrats and Republicans are going to ratify radical ideas? I double any foolish Amendments will be presented, but they will be dead on arrival.

4. The resolution proposed in this book sets high standards for all delegates who attend the Convention. They cannot have any influence from Washington. The resolution also prohibits changes in our Bill of Rights, civil rights, or the creation of privileges. Most important, it gives guidance as to the changes that are needed.

5. Finally, do you like what is going on in our government now? The trend in Washington is making things worse. Presidents abuse the Constitution. Congress is dysfunctional. The Supreme Court stretches the meaning of our Constitution. Do we want these trends to continue? Let's use the opportunity granted

by our Founding Fathers! A Convention is not only the *best* way it is the *only* way to Repair Washington. We have no other choice and the need for action is urgent! We have serious problems.

Are you concerned about our huge National Debt? Are you in favor of two-term limits? Are elections too long and costly? Do you feel we need citizen patriots in Congress? Does our free press keep us fully informed? Do criminals get better protection than their victims? Is tort reform overdue? Should we have financial discipline? Shouldn't more than nine large states elect the President? Do you think Congress will ever address these and other important needed changes?

**A properly organized Constitutional Convention can address all these issues and more. It can restore functional government in Washington.**

Our Founding Fathers created the United States as a *republic*. In our Pledge of Allegiance to the Flag we say, "and to the Republic for which it stands." We started as a republic and have evolved into a democracy. This book does not propose we return to a republic, but it is clear that we need to reduce the size of our government. It has become so large and expensive that it is transitioning into a socialistic bureaucracy where agencies act beyond the powers granted by Congress. Spending, debts, and deficits are soaring without discipline. The people are burdened with wasteful high taxes and regulations that limit our freedoms, opportunities and prosperity. Economic growth is slow, good jobs are scarce, and the American Dream is fading.

Today's professional politicians are an elite club expecting to be reelected for life. Their benefits are self-ordained and they exempt themselves from laws we must follow. Of necessity they must serve the *special interests* that finance their campaigns that get them reelected over and over. The corruption is outrageous and our press does not keep citizens informed. The few patriots in Congress are overwhelmed by party politics, the seniority system, and the corruption.

Over the last several decades the United States has slowly lost leadership in many fields we formerly dominated. We are not the only free people. Of the 207 nations in this world, 180 are considered free, so freedom alone is insufficient for greatness. We have slipped to $7^{th}$ in literacy, $7^{th}$ in competitiveness, $31^{st}$ in math, $21^{st}$ in reading, $24^{th}$ in science, $49^{th}$ in life expectancy, $4^{th}$ in quality of labor force, $178^{th}$ in infant mortality, $3^{rd}$ in median household income, and $4^{th}$ in exports. Asia is taking the lead by using the Free Enterprise System that we are slowly abandoning.

With repeated increases in taxes, spending, and regulations, our growing federal government has produced a steady decline in the quality of life for the working people, with excessive concentration of wealth in the top politically connected 1%. Trillions of dollars have failed to reduce poverty. We have the highest per capita number of people in jail and a military larger than any other country of the world. We are first in the cost of medical care but 50th in the quality of care. It is indeed time for a change.

## A PRUDENT RESOLUTION

There are many patriotic Americans who wish to call a single issue Convention. One group wants a Balanced Budget Amendment, and another a Countermand Amendment. That is too limiting because so many changes are needed to update our Constitution. Thus a single issue Constitution is likely "bolt" and become a "run away" Convention. That doesn't worry me because the ratification process is so stringent an imprudent Amendment will never be ratified.

Doesn't it make better sense to proscribe what delegates cannot do, and what we want them to do so that many needed Amendments can be offered for ratification to improve our nation? The resolution proposed here does this and includes an amendment to restore financial discipline, and an improved Countermand Amendment, term limits and much more. A Constitutional Convention is legal and should be charged to offer many Amendments to modernize our government, and let the ratification process make the decision.

An open Convention can propose term limits, shorter elections, set campaign contribution limits and establish governmental ethics. Candidates should be personally responsible for all of their advertising and publicity. Laws that apply to citizens should also apply to elected officials, and vice-versa. We need to proscribe punishments for elected officials and government employees who breach their public trust. Our free press should also be responsible for being *truthful* and respectful of citizens' *privacy*. Litigation and tax reform are overdue. Why not clarify what is, and is not a crime, and indict, prosecute, sentence, and punish violent criminals promptly to remove them as a danger to the public? And how about budget discipline?

New Constitutional Amendments should refocus our government on what we need it to do and prohibit it from doing that which citizens can do better for ourselves. We need to encourage citizen independence and self-reliance rather than dependence on government. The time has come to reestablish responsive government and enjoy what our government was founded to do, *provide the freedoms of life, liberty and the pursuit of happiness.*

The resolution proposed is unique because it also addresses the structure and organization of a Convention. It seeks to replicate the same conditions that existed at the original Constitutional Convention. The Convention must be called, organized, and financed by the states. The United States did not exist at our original Convention, and must be excluded again so that successful change can be achieved.

These realistic and exciting opportunities are available only if we call a Constitutional Convention. Without a Convention, the amendments in this book are not worth the paper they are written on.

Inspiring our state legislatures to call a Constitutional Convention will not be easy, but it is the **only legal method** available to amend our Constitution and restore responsive government. Congress will NEVER do it.

**The purpose of this book is to offer a user-friendly practical resolution so that 34 states will pass it and call a Constitutional Convention! We need new amendments to restore our freedoms, opportunities, and prosperity! Please help call a CONSTITUTIONAL CONVENTION!**

# THE REPAIR WASHINGTON RESOLUTION
## A CONTINUING RESOLUTION TO CALL A CONVENTION TO SUCCESSFULLY AMEND THE CONSTITUTION

*"Human rights preexist government."*

James Madison

It is very important to understand the unique power structure of our U.S. Government. We are a self-governed people. Power comes from the people bottom up, not from Kings or Queens top down. All political power rests with us except those limited powers we have granted to the states. The states have granted limited powers to our central government by calling and ratifying the Constitution. The states created the United States of America. Citizens have never voted on the Constitution or any amendments.

In the over 227 years since the United States came into existence the federal central government has gradually taken more and more power from the states, and from the people. Now a politicized Supreme Court unilaterally interprets the Constitution and further centralizes power in ways never intended. These changes may prove harmful to our freedoms and opportunities.

Elected officials in Washington will not reverse this trend but seek to enhance their powers. The last amendment passed in 1992 authorized the Congress to determine its own pay and benefits. The previous amendment in 1971 gave 18-year citizens the right to vote. That was 43 years ago. Now Congress is working on an amendment that would give them control over federal elections presently controlled by the states. Our Constitution has not been kept current with the rapid progress of civilization.

Since Washington will not repair itself, we must use the legal powers of the states and the Constitution that permit convening another Constitutional Convention. This can be achieved if two-thirds of the states (34) pass resolutions calling for a convention. A resolution is like any law where a majority vote of the house and senate approve it, but it does not require the signature of the governor.

### LIMITING AND GUIDING THE CONVENTION'S POWERS

There is justified concern about this process. We must limit the powers of convention delegates. This resolution is designed to do that on many levels. This resolution specifically prohibits any amendments from "altering the Bill of Rights, limiting civil rights, reducing personal freedom, or creating special privileges." We want only a positive outcome. We urgently need a Convention or it is certain our freedoms and opportunities will be continually reduced. There is another concern.

Our Constitution requires that the resolution instruct the U.S. Congress to convene the Convention. The members of Congress will not want a Convention. They know that popular two-term limits will be proposed and ratified by the states. That puts most of them out of office, and they will try to prevent that from happening. If their powers in calling the Convention are not limited they could delay it or fill it with their allies. The resolution below prevents this by only permitted Congress to *promptly set the date for the convention and nothing else.*

More importantly, the resolution defines the positive things that need to be achieved. It reads, *"Amendments shall address term limits, election procedures and reform, ethics for public servants, financial discipline, a countermand amendment, and other appropriate matters to modernize the Constitution and enhance the freedoms, opportunities, and prosperity of the people."*

Since it will take time, perhaps years before enough states pass this resolution, it must be a "continuing resolution," and it is best if the states pass reasonably similar resolutions. Hopefully the "Repair Washington Resolution" proposed here will prove friendly to many legislatures. Its objective is to recreate conditions similar to those that were so successful at our original Constitutional Constitution. This resolution is carefully structured to maximize success.

The format below is used for resolutions in my state, Louisiana. It lists the title, sponsors, a summary, and then the specifics. It can be easily revised to achieve sufficient votes for passage in other states. Please read it carefully as well as the explanation that follows. It is designed to give a rebirth of freedom and opportunities, especially for the future of our young citizens.

### THE REPAIR WASHINGTON RESOLUTION
### A CONTINUING RESOLUTION TO CALL A CONVENTION TO SUCCESSFULLY AMEND THE CONSTITUTION

**BY:** *(sponsors for Louisiana's Legislature in April 2015)*
**U.S. CONSTITUTION:** *Applies and orders the U.S. Congress to promptly convene a Constitutional Convention on a specific date, leaving all other decisions and powers to the state legislatures and their appointed delegates as to the location, qualifications for delegates, procedures, and finances as provided for herein. The Constitutional Convention shall propose amendments for ratification by the states as part of the Constitution. Delegates are prohibited and instructed to oppose amendments that alter the Bill of Rights, limit civil rights, reduce personal freedoms, or create special privileges. Amendments shall address term limits, election procedures and reform, ethics for public servants, financial discipline, a Countermand Amendment, and other appropriate matters to modernize the Constitution and enhance the freedoms, opportunities, and prosperity of the people.*

**WHEREAS** *political power is vested with the People, and*

**WHEREAS** *the People have consented to self-government by granting limited powers to the States, and*

**WHEREAS** *the States ordered the original Constitutional Convention, and*

**WHEREAS** *the States ratified the proposed Constitution thus creating a central government called the United States of America and granting to it limited powers, and*

**WHEREAS** *Article V of that Constitution as well as the powers granted to the States by the People permit the calling of another Constitutional Convention, and*

**WHEREAS** *most cities update their charters every few decades, and States update their Constitutions about every 100 years, and the United States Constitution has not been updated for over 235 years, and*

**WHEREAS** *the calling of a Constitutional Convention is legal, long overdue and urgently needed,*

**THEREFORE BE IT RESOLVED** *that the Legislature of Louisiana does hereby apply to and order the United States Congress to promptly, within thirty days of the two-thirds (34) of the state legislatures having passed this or similar resolutions, promptly set the date for the convening of a Constitutional Convention, such date being no sooner than five months or later than six months from* the date of that two-thirds event, and further that Congress, the President and Supreme Court have no powers or authority other than to set that date; and should the Congress fail to promptly comply, the States and/or their delegations are authorized to act independently, as is their right, to take such action as necessary to convene the Convention.

**BE IT FURTHER RESOLVED** that Delegates are prohibited and are instructed to oppose amendments that alter the Bill of Rights, limit civil rights, reduce any freedoms of the People, or in any way create special privileges.

**BE IT FURTHER RESOLVED THAT THE OBJECTIVES OF THE CONVENTION ARE** to recommend Amendments to the United States Constitution that shall, if ratified, make our national government more responsive to the long-term best interests and freedoms of all citizens by addressing term limits, election procedures and reform, ethics for public servants, financial discipline, a Countermand Amendment, and other appropriate changes to the United States Government that will modernize the Constitution and expand the opportunities and prosperity of the people. The Convention rules of order will seek to emulate the conditions present at the First Constitutional Convention by providing security, privacy, and procedures for open discussion that encourage neither haste nor delay, wise decisions, and recommendations of acceptable amendments.

## BE IT FURTHER RESOLVED

**STATE DELEGATIONS AND DELEGATES.** *Each state may send a Delegation to the Convention. Each Delegation shall have one vote, equal rights, privileges, authority, and all else necessary to accomplish the Convention's Objectives. Each state may, in any manner it sees fit, elect or appoint no less than three and no more than seven Official Delegates to represent their state's interests at the convention. Two Alternate Delegates may be elected to substitute for any Official Delegates unable to serve for any reason.*

**QUALIFICATIONS FOR OFFICIAL DELEGATES AND ALTERNATES.** *Delegates and alternates must be United States citizens, no less than 40 years of age, and with a reputation for honesty, hard work, intelligence, and patriotism. No person shall be eligible to serve as a Delegate if he or she is serving or has been in the Federal Government in any elected, judicial, appointed or employed position; nor has ever been convicted as a felon, declared bankruptcy, or been employed as a lobbyist. The Convention may select non-voting advisors that may include past Presidents of the United States and active members of our Armed Forces, subject to the same qualifications as Official Delegates.*

**ORGANIZATION.** *After no less than 20 Delegations have been empowered by their state, a temporary convening committee shall be appointed from those states to determine where, and if necessary when* (should Congress fail to promptly do so), the Convention shall convene, certify the qualifications of all Delegates, provide credentials, and make all necessary arrangements to convene the Convention.

Upon convening, the Convention shall elect the Administrative Committee charged with the full responsibility for the operation and rules of order for the Convention. The Administrative Committee is further empowered to discharge any Delegate for cause, or breach of secrecy or security, or conflict of interest; however a majority vote of the Convention may at any time overrule a decision of the Administrative Committee, and change any of its members

At no time will any Delegation be denied its right and responsibility to represent its state by voting on every motion and amendment. Any absence of one or more Official Delegates from a Delegation shall not deny that Delegation its right to vote. Should the Administrative Committee disqualify any Official Delegate, the next Alternate Delegate from that state shall immediately fill their place with full authority.

**FINANCE.** The cost for the operation of the Constitutional Convention shall be borne equally among all states. To cover Convention operations, every state shall promptly send no less than two million dollars to officially install their Delegation. Additional requests for funds shall be borne equally among all the states and shall be paid promptly, or their Delegation may not vote.

*Within forty-five days after the Convention is adjourned, all financial obligations are to be promptly settled with a full accounting of all costs presented to every state, and all remaining funds equally distributed among the states.*

*Each state shall bear all of the personal and living expenses of its Official and Alternate Delegates.*

**PRIVACY and SECURITY.** *The Convention shall appoint a Security Committee charged with the responsibility and authority to maintain privacy, security, secrecy, and assure that all Convention activities, meetings, communications, documents and conversations shall be confidential. It will foster conditions for thoughtful and respectful communications between Official Delegates, and working conditions conducive to the origination of prudent, practical, and politically acceptable Amendments for ratification.*

*The committee shall prohibit members of the press, lobbyists, and any unauthorized persons from coming in or near the venue, subject to arrest for trespassing, fine of $100,000, and imprisonment for no less than one year at the cost of and with the cooperation of the state in which the Convention is held.*

*The committee shall have full authority to select and employ reliable security forces sufficient to provide the necessary safety, secrecy and security of all Delegates.*

**PATRIOTISM.** *All Official Delegates to the Convention shall take the following oath. "I swear to faithfully serve the American People by fulfilling my duties as a delegate*

Within forty-five days after the Convention is adjourned, all financial obligations are to be promptly settled with a full accounting of all costs presented to every state, and all remaining funds equally distributed among the states.

Each state shall bear all of the personal and living expenses of its Official and Alternate Delegates.

**PRIVACY and SECURITY.** The Convention shall appoint a Security Committee charged with the responsibility and authority to maintain privacy, security, secrecy, and assure that all Convention activities, meetings, communications, documents and conversations shall be confidential. It will foster conditions for thoughtful and respectful communications between Official Delegates, and working conditions conducive to the origination of prudent, practical, and politically acceptable Amendments for ratification.

The committee shall prohibit members of the press, lobbyists, and any unauthorized persons from coming in or near the venue, subject to arrest for trespassing, fine of $100,000, and imprisonment for no less than one year at the cost of and with the cooperation of the state in which the Convention is held.

The committee shall have full authority to select and employ reliable security forces sufficient to provide the necessary safety, secrecy and security of all Delegates.

**PATRIOTISM.** All Official Delegates to the Convention shall take the following oath. "I swear to faithfully serve the American People by fulfilling my duties as a Delegate *to this Convention. I promise to respect and cooperate with other Delegates, work with patriotism, and recommend amendments for the betterment of the nation, so help me God."*

*Delegations shall work with reasonable expedition presenting Amendments to the states for ratification only after all of the work is complete, said Amendments having been approved by a majority of the Delegations at adjournment of the Convention.*

**BE IT FURTHER RESOLVED** *that the Louisiana secretary of state is hereby directed to transmit copies of this resolution to the president and secretary of the United States Senate and the speaker and clerk of the United States House of Representatives, and copies hereof to the presiding officers of each of the legislative houses of the several states, requesting their cooperation.*

**BE IT FURTHER RESOLVED** *that this resolution constitutes a continuing application in accordance with Article V of the Constitution of the United States until the legislatures of at least two-thirds of the several states have passed such resolutions.*

## EXPLANATION

**INTRODUCTION**. This resolution is short, precise, and hopefully would appeal to 34 state legislatures needed to call the Convention. *To make sure the conditions in Washington do not reproduce themselves at a Constitutional Convention, the qualifications of Delegates* *preclude anyone who has been elected, appointed, or served the Federal Government except past Presidents.*

**DELEGATES TO THE CONVENTION.** The original Constitutional Convention representing 13 states had 55 Delegates, and 34 did most of the work. That size well represented the 13 states but is too small for 50 states.

What is the right number that is not too big nor too small and is most likely to duplicate conditions similar to our original Constitutional Convention? What number will have sufficient diversity to faithfully represent a cross section of the outlook, philosophy and dreams of the American People? What number would most likely produce success?

This resolution permits each state to select in its own manner no less than three and no more than seven Delegates. Official delegates could include the governor, majority and minority leaders of the state House and Senate, and perhaps two mayors. The choices are wide open.

The Convention would assemble no more than 350 and no less than 150 Delegates for the Convention. Surely that range should include a large enough number from across the nation to represent each state and the attitude of the American People. When the Convention is over, we will need a goodly number of delegates to go back to their legislature and population to encourage ratification of the new Amendments.

**DELEGATE QUALIFICATIONS**. Delegates should be bright, honest, and respected *patriots*, who can represent the American people *without the slightest possibility of conflicts of interest.* Influence from Washington are excluded.

**FINANCES**. Each state provides the initial two million dollars (a total of $100 million) for the central operation of the Convention. Also, each state will be directly responsible for the expenses of its delegates. This will provide the Convention with adequate resources to operate smoothly as it may last several months. Delegates will need good meeting and dining facilities, privacy, security and personal accommodations. This financial approach will make sure the Convention is independent of the federal government. When the Convention adjourns all funds spent should be accounted for, and unspent funds promptly divided equally among all the states.

**ADMINISTRATION**. An Administrative Committee is needed to supervise the operations of the Convention, set dates, times, establish rules of order, and prevent influence from special interests. It will have authority to appoint a staff sufficient to provide all necessary services.

**PRIVACY AND SECRECY.** The delegates who wrote our Constitution held their deliberations in secrecy. Only when they finished their work did they disclose the proposed Constitutional document for public review and ratification by the states. That prevented outside interference in the discussions, and created conditions whereby the best outcome could be achieved.

We must be mindful of First Amendment rights of the press. In this instance the press could delay, interfere, and even embarrass open constructive discussion. Once the work of the Convention is complete, full disclosure of recommendations and events should be made available, but not until the work is complete.

All Convention meetings, discussions, and conversations should be held in private to replicate conditions for thoughtful and respectful discussions to produce good results. Delegates who breach this moral obligation should be promptly dismissed from the Convention. The press and lobbyists must be specifically prohibited from the campus of the Convention and facilities of the Delegates. No reports should be made to the public until the Convention has completed its work, and the Delegates have signed and forwarded the recommended Amendments to their respective state legislatures for ratification.

The Security Committee shall provide privacy, safety, security, and hire sufficient staff to ensure these services.

**VENUE.** The delegations should appoint a temporary committee to choose the venue and certify Official Delegates.

**ETHICS**. No group or persons should be permitted to engrave an Amendment advantageous to any special interests into Amendments. Amendments that limit freedoms, civil rights, or create special privileges must be prohibited. Despite every precaution, it is possible that outside influences may seek to guide members of the Convention to act in favor of special interests, breach confidentiality, or stretch ethics. The Administrative Committee must be alert and have sufficient power to prevent this from happening, and if necessary immediately disqualify any Delegate or advisor.

## IN SUMMARY

This legislation should motivate our state legislatures to call a Convention. One obvious incentive is that two-term limits will open doors to patriotic men and women who otherwise would never get the opportunity to serve our country.

"We the People" must speak! An enthusiastic and determined grass-roots push from the citizens is essential if a Convention is ever to be called. As Ronald Reagan said, "Government is not the solution, government is the problem."

Life, liberty, and the pursuit of happiness must be earned by each generation. Too many have died to protect our freedoms. If we fail to restore, strengthen and protect our freedoms we will have failed our children and grandchildren.

*We need to update our Constitution **NOW!** Let's make it happen!*

# WHAT WENT WRONG?

*"Experience hath shown, that even under the best forms (of government) those entrusted with power have, in time, and by slow operations, perverted it into tyranny. I am not a friend to a very energetic government. It is always oppressive. The course of history shows that as a government grows, liberty decreases. Government big enough to supply everything you need is big enough to take everything you have."*

Thomas Jefferson

*"Television will change our lives more in the next five years than in the last fifty."*

Brian Roberts, Chairman & CEO Comcast

How has Washington gone awry? Is it the politicians' fault? Not entirely. Extraordinary fundamental changes in healthcare and technology that our Founding Fathers could not possibly anticipate have caused our government to become inefficient, dysfunctional, and yes, corrupt.

In the 1780's when the Constitution was framed the estimated average life expectancy was 46. Back then age 35 was an elder statesman. Our Founding Fathers could not possibly anticipate today's average life expectancy of 79. That was an inconceivable dream, even absurd. The writers of our Constitution expected citizen patriots to serve in our government for no more than one or two terms at most. Indeed for over 150 years, half or more of the Congress turned over in every election.

In Washington, we now endure professional career politicians serving for 20, 30, and even 40-years. Representative John Dingell, Democrat from Michigan since 1955, has announced his retirement after serving for 49 years. He found today's Congress "obnoxious."

Professional politicians make millions for themselves by following the party line and wheeling and dealing with lobbyists. They have also made our elections long, costly, and brutal, to help themselves get reelected over and over.

In the past community leaders, successful businessmen, doctors, farmers, people of good and honorable reputation were asked by their peers to go to Washington to serve our country. It was a personal and financial sacrifice. Friends had to send money monthly so that those who served would not become financially embarrassed. Today, professional politicians make millions, live and travel high at government expense. Elections against entrenched incumbents are so long, expensive, and vicious that the most qualified people will not subject themselves to that abuse. The quality of our leadership has declined.

Running for office is a full time money-raising job 24/7 for well over a year. Day after day, candidates have two and three breakfasts, two or three lunches, and a couple of dinners to raise money. Those who donate big money have inappropriate influence and control on how our government is run after the election.

Congress plays at election reform but genuine reform will only come from a Constitutional Convention. Amendments for term limits, the length of elections, and limits on political donations are urgently needed to correct this situation. Those recommendations for your consideration are in this book.

A paradigm technological change occurred in the 1960 Presidential election that drastically revolutionized American politics forever. Our Founding Fathers could not anticipate the invention of television. Today, showmanship on TV, rather than performance, talent, and leadership -- wins elections.

The key event was the 1960 Presidential campaign between Richard Nixon, the Republican Vice President under a very popular President Dwight Eisenhower, and an unknown Catholic Democrat, John Kennedy, an inexperienced junior senator from Massachusetts. Well known, respected and supported by President Eisenhower, Vice President Nixon was well ahead in the polls and a sure winner. John Kennedy was expected to lose.

Their campaign featured the first *televised* Presidential debate. It was in *black and white* because Color TV had not yet been invented. Tens of millions watched, the largest audience ever, and it changed history.

It wasn't really a debate; it was a charm and popularity contest. No real issues were argued, and no solutions were tendered. It was nice-sounding rhetoric and no one remembered any content other than his or her *emotional responses* to the visible talking heads on the screen. Nixon needed a shave and looked grim. Kennedy's youth, flowing hair, Boston accent and charismatic image soared. Overnight an unknown candidate became a winner.

The radio listeners to the debate, who could not **see** the candidates, thought that Nixon won handily, but the visual impact of TV was so powerful that polls taken the very next day projected Kennedy would win the Presidency – and he did.

This was the first time Americans could actually see and react to the personality of a live candidate on a TV screen. It immediately became clear that TV was so powerful that elections could be won if you had enough money and ran the right spots! Wisdom, experience, and leadership capability were relegated to charm, looks, charisma, and smooth talk. Quickly, all candidates started raising money to win elections with TV. *Television* has changed American politics forever!

Today, every politician's TV image is professionally packaged to appear handsome or beautiful, sound trustworthy, and say nothing that offends anyone. It is choreographed entertainment. Truth is stretched, ignored, and too often trampled. Candidates spew good-sounding rhetoric without any specific content. They viciously attack opponents, promise everything, *offer no real solutions,* and **win**.

We never really get to know the candidates' quali-fications, only their carefully packaged images. It has become a cruel and manipulative popularity contest. With enough money for TV, a reasonably good-looking, verbally savvy, inexperienced incompetent person can run for any office and win.

Negative, even untrue attacks on TV are effective, and not in the interest of the public. In the last couple of days of his Presidential campaign Lyndon Johnson ran TV spots showing an atomic explosion claiming that a vote for Barry Goldwater increased the risk of atomic war. The spot was bogus and clearly untrue. Yet it frightened voters enough for Johnson to won. Lyndon Johnson was a great legislator but not a good admin-istrator and failed to get enough support for a second term. Would Goldwater have served our country better?

Who has the millions of dollars for TV spots? Certainly not the average voter. Big money comes from many "special interests." Giant corporations that have big government contracts, donate heavily and repeat-edly. Private interests in need of self-serving legislation donate heavily, and even foreign interests buy influ-ence with money. Hundreds of millions of dollars are funneled through lobbyists who obligate candidates and control how elected officials vote <u>after the election</u>.

The process of collecting the money is secret. The July 16th 2012 issue of *Business Week* reported that a $50,000-per-person dinner fundraiser was held for Presidential candidate Mitt Romney with tight security at the home of billionaire David Koch. The magazine wrote, "We don't know what Romney told guests at Chez Koch, because, like most fundraisers at supporters' homes, it was off-limits to all but those opening deep wallets. As usual, journalists were kept at a safe distance and the campaign wouldn't release Romney's remarks."

Continuing with *Business Week*, "President Obama was just as tightlipped about his lavish fundraising dinners. His handlers allow reporters to witness boilerplate-opening remarks before herding them to the curb. But President Obama was so determined to make sure there's no record of his less formal comments, campaign workers confiscated guests' phones and put them in plastic bags before some fundraisers."

What are the secrets that the public is not permitted to know? **<u>The truth is that elections have become an advance sale of public monies and benefits for special interests.</u>** After the election the voters are forgotten, except for feeding us more nice sounding "spin." We just pay the bills.

Before the Nixon/Kennedy debate, there were about 4,000 lobbyists in Washington. In 2011, 12,220 lobbyists spent $2.45 billion to influence our government. It is estimated that total funds raised for the 2012 combined Presidential and Congressional races approached six billion dollars. That $6 billion obligated our $3.8 trillion budget to the interests of the donors.

Lobbyists wield long-term power! A congressman or senator has to remember their big donors and protect their interests. Failure to vote as the lobbyists want, means that in the next election, the big money will go to his or her opponent. Thus, *once elected, they are more obligated to the lobbyists and special interests than to the interests of the people!* Thanks to television's impact on today's elections, the lobbyists are now our *phantom* legislators. The special interests who provide the money are the "citizens" to whom our government responds.

Special interests include, labor unions, civil service employees, businesses, including those that administer social programs, military contractors, bankers, large and small government contractors, Wall Street interests, attorneys, CPAs, energy companies, AARP, foreign countries, foreign businesses, wealthy citizens and many more. With up-front money, they get what they want in Washington. Everything is for sale because our politicians want to become rich. Our government is largely run for their political benefit and we citizens and future generations pay their bills.

Most Americans instinctively know that something is broken in Washington. Now you know what it is.

Former Democratic Senator, Evan Bayh, decided not to run for reelection to the Senate because he felt money raising had become his full-time job. He lamented that when his dad was in the Senate he would run for two years and govern for four. Now Congress focuses on two things: raising money by exchanging influence for cash, and statistical advice from pollsters that can get them reelected. Neither are sources for sound legislation or the long-term future betterment of the United States. The system works so that politicians get reelected over and over again. That's why we have "professional politicians" instead of citizen patriots.

Today, legislators obligated to special interests repeatedly produce deficits and have accumulated a huge national debt that has become a serious drag on our nation's growth. Future unfunded benefits represent many more additional trillions that will burden our children in the years to come. Professional politicians cannot afford budget discipline because they must pay back the special interests that got them elected.

Legislators assure their reelection by promising voters with well-intended "free entitlements" that have caused destructive social changes. These laws have weakened the family unit, lowered moral values, encouraged the birth of out-of-wedlock children, weakened the work ethic, undermined the quality of education, and increased crime.

The spending has a cycle: - spend, produce a deficit, raise taxes, spend into another deficit, raise more taxes ---- over and over.

We are also burdened with complex and expensive regulations that deter job creation. Government has placed such a heavy burden on small businesses that economic growth is anemic. We have the lowest percentage of working population in over two decades.

Another very destructive political procedure made possible by the professional politicians is the "seniority system." Now, rather than competence, the *length of time in office* determines who shall be Committee Chairpersons.

The arrogant attitude of professional politicians also permeates our federal courts. Our courts go beyond interpreting the Constitution. They write legislation. As you read on you will see that our courts are politicized.

Our Founding Fathers did not want royalty or a small elite group ruling our nation. Today Congress **is** indeed an <u>elite club</u> that has passed laws that set the Congress above the people in benefits and privilege. These benefits, by mutual agreement between the two political parties, are kept secret.

**Professional politicians will not make any changes that would reduce or limit their POWERS. Only Amendments to our Constitution can Repair Washington!**

**WE NEED TO WRITE, PHONE, EMAIL, DO EVERYTHING POSSIBLE TO ENCOURAGE OUR ELECTED STATE LEADERS TO PASS RESOLUTIONS TO CALL A CONSTITUTIONAL CONVENTION!**

# TWO CONSTITUTIONAL SITUATIONS

When our wise Founding Fathers wrote our Constitution the political environment was different from today. Our first government was the Continental Congress. It was loosely organized, had few sources of revenue, little political power, and failed. In three years its currency, called the Continental, became worthless and unacceptable in trade because it was printed in unlimited quantities. Those who attended the Constitutional Convention had experienced that collapse and they would not repeat those mistakes.

In Europe, royal families and their courts owned most of the land. They were the only people who were free to do what they wanted, and the common man had few rights. Prior attempts to weaken the feudal systems failed. The most famous was the Magna Carta forced on King John in 1215. These prior efforts had little political success. Amazingly, our revolutionary Constitution and the "Bill of Rights" represented a radical political innovation that changed the world!

Between May 15, 1787 and September 17, 1787, working diligently for four months, the Constitutional

Convention completed the blueprint for a remarkable, innovative new kind of government, a *republic*! It was financially solvent, with balances of power, and introduced the totally new concepts of "personal freedom" which ultimately produced the "Free Enterprise System."

When the state legislatures ratified it, The United States Constitution became the supreme law of the land. The first U.S. Congress met on March 4, 1789 in New York City and immediately approved <u>twelve</u> Amendments to the Constitution. On December 15, 1791 the states ratified only the first ten Amendments called the "Bill of Rights."

—

Today, political conditions are significantly different. Many diverse ingredients have been added to our American "melting pot" in over two centuries. Our economy has grown and the American People have created great prosperity and astounding innovations.

It took several Amendments over many years to gradually enlarging our voting base. Women could not vote until the 19th Amendment in 1920. The 26th Amendment to our Constitution was ratified on July 1, 1971, 43 years ago! It guaranteed the right for citizens eighteen years of age or older to vote. That was the last legitimate change to our Constitution.

Amendment XXVII, ratified May 7, 1992, read, "No law, varying the compensation for the services of the Senators and Representatives, shall take effect until an election of Representatives shall have intervened." This permitted Congress to decide its own payments and benefits, to be implemented after the next election. Since our Representatives are permanent career professional politicians, they have given themselves secret benefits far beyond those of the citizens.

Professional career politicians are in control because Constitutional change is paralyzed. It has been 43 years since Congress has proposed a new Amendment to keep our Constitution current despite the rapid changes taking place in our world. Power corrupts and absolute power is on the way.

Our government has gradually transitioned from being a servant of the People into our Master. Through taxation, regulations, and influence from special interests, freedom and opportunity are gradually being gathered into the hands of a small elite club in Washington with a Socialistic agenda and powerful special interests.

To get reelected over and over, our career politicians increasingly move our economy toward the failed Socialistic economic model that destroyed the Soviet Union, pauperized Cuba, and provided both poverty and starvation in North Korea. Socialism does not eliminate poverty; it increases it. When voters who enjoy free entitlements expand beyond the voters who work to produce the wealth Free Enterprise fades and disappears. We are getting close to that transition.

The bigger and more powerful our government, the more it will protect us from the freedoms of life, liberty and the pursuit of happiness.

## TEN AMENDMENTS

<u>Only</u> a Constitutional Convention will propose amendments that can Repair Washington. The ten Amendments suggested here are for the consideration of Our Constitutional Convention. They are written in a style similar to our Constitution. Each Article of our Constitution has several Sections that describe policies, concepts, limits, or definitions. There is an explanation for the rationale for each Section of each Amendment.

The first three Amendments relate to the "process" by which we select public servants and their performance requirement. I view them as critically important: term limits, short elections with limitations on who can donate, and ethics. The remaining seven Amendments are areas of "reform" to improve social, legal, criminal, and economic conditions. They are submitted in an effort to explore all opportunities. Our Constitutional Convention will decide their merit, if any.

For your convenience all Amendments are in larger print with every section appearing at the beginning of each chapter and then followed by an explanation with that section repeated.

Some of these Amendment concepts are well known and popular with most Americans. Two term limits is an example. Some are original, exciting, and surprising. <u>Any and every idea that might have any potential value has been included for consideration by our Constitutional Convention</u>.

I have no pride of authorship. Please believe me, all the ideas presented are intended to improve the performance of our government for the benefit of the people. A Constitutional Convention will determine their merit.

There are not enough ways for me to emphasize that <u>without a Constitutional Convention</u>, changes for the better WILL <u>NEVER</u> HAPPEN.

# Chapter One

# TERM LIMITS

## Section 1. ONE SIX-YEAR PRESIDENTIAL TERM

The twelfth and twenty-second articles of Amendment to the Constitution of the United States are hereby repealed.

The President and Vice President shall serve for one term of six years in their lifetime. A Vice President who shall serve in the office for more than three years shall not be eligible to run for the office of President. The President and Vice President must be no less than 45 years of age to qualify for the office.

## Section 2. TWO TERM LIMITS FOR CONGRESS

The term of office for members of the House of Representatives shall be for three years, and no persons may serve in the House of Representatives for more than six years in their lifetime. No person may serve in the Senate for more than twelve years in their lifetime.

Let's begin with the term of the President. The British political system uses ministerial positions to train potential future Prime Ministers. The United States provides little training for the office of President. During the first 12 to 18 months on the job, a new President is in a steep learning curve. Just as the President learns how to manage the executive responsibilities, mid-term elections and then his own reelection absorbs valuable time and attention.

One six-year Presidential term will focus our nation's CEO on making the right long-term decisions for our country during their entire time in office. Since they will never stand for reelection, they can go to the People to sell their ideas and focus on making a favorable record for history.

At the time the Constitution was written, with an average life expectancy of 46, the age defined to qualify to President was set at 35. With today's extended life expectancy, we need a more mature age to qualify to run for President and Vice President. Today, a person age 45 is entering his or her prime productive years and has had time to have established a good reputation, accumulated experience, and demonstrated a track record of administrative excellence. Again, here is Section 1.

## **Section 1.** ONE SIX-YEAR PRESIDENTIAL TERM

The twelfth and twenty-second articles of Amendment to the Constitution of the United States are hereby repealed.

The President and Vice President shall serve for one term of six years in their lifetime. A Vice President who shall serve in the office for more than three years shall not be eligible to run for the office of President. The President and Vice President must be no less than 45 years of age to qualify for the office.

Now let's take a look at Congress. Two-term limits are essential if we are to repair Washington. Two-term limits will break the tight hold that special interests and the seniority system have on our government.

Because two-term limits will "clean house," such an Amendment will only come from a Constitutional Convention, not Congress.

Electing younger patriot citizens into government will restore genuine patriotism to our Congress. Limited terms focuses elected officials on running the government for the benefit of the people rather than to get reelected. Because they cannot make it a career they are likely to vote for what is right in the long term, even if unpopular. Where cities and states have enacted term limits, the quality of elected officials and their performance has improved. In Louisiana and New Orleans, two-term limits at both the state and city levels have forced out the "good old boys" and put many qualified people into office.

Once among the most corrupt states in the nation, Louisiana and New Orleans have turned around. In New Orleans, Mayor Mitch Landrieu, City Council members, and District Attorney Leon Cannizaro are among the best leadership we have enjoyed in decades. Our city is booming. At the state level our legislature is more responsible because the "good old boys" are gone.

Another reason that two term limits are needed is because TV has made it very difficult to unseat incumbents. Regular vacancies opening will attract unknown but qualified candidates who will look upon elected office as public service rather than a career. But term limits alone will not fully repair Washington.

Let's start with the House of Representatives. House members presently serve for only two years. They spend their first year in a learning curve; the second year they are running for reelection. House members are pretty much running for office all the time. Two years is too short.

Why not change the term for representatives to three years, and then limit them to two terms only, for a total of six years? A three-year term means that new representatives could devote their second year to good work without the distraction of running for office. If reelected for a second term, all three years would be free of election pressure so they could focus on doing a good job. This should change the entire outlook of the House of Representatives just as it has improved state legislatures.

If we enact a six-year Presidential term, but don't change the two-year term for representatives, the President would be distracted by two interim Congressional elections. If we change the term for the

House from two years to <u>three years</u>, there would be only one mid-term election during each Presidency.

Senators would be limited to two, six-year terms, or a maximum of twelve years in their lifetime.

Arguments against term limits ring hollow, and are mostly designed to protect the dysfunctional status quo.

## **Section 2.** TWO TERM LIMITS FOR CONGRESS

The term of office for members of the House of Representatives shall be for three years, and no persons may serve in the House of Representatives for more than six years in their lifetime. No person may serve in the Senate for more than twelve years in their lifetime.

# Chapter Two

# ELECTION REFORM

This Amendment is tough, and needs to be tough. It is intended to clean up elections and restore power to the citizens. It shortens elections, greatly reduces their cost, proscribes ethical ways to raise campaign money, and emphasizes the positive attributes of each candidate. It also significantly reduces and limits the power of lobbyists, corporations, unions, Political Action Committees, and special interests to obligate and influence elected officials after the election. Foreign influence is removed from our elections, gerrymandering ends, and the Electoral College is updated.

Most important, elected officials shall enter office without being compromised in their ability to focus on the long-term best interests of the nation.

## Section 1. CANDIDATE QUALIFICATIONS

All candidates seeking federal office must be American citizens.

### **Section 2.** ONLY CITIZENS CAN VOTE

Only registered citizens of the United States may vote and must provide proof of identity when voting. States may choose to require that voting, subject to penalty, is mandatory.

### **Section 3.** SIX-WEEK PRIMARIES AND ELECTIONS

All primary and general elections shall be for no more than six weeks. Primary elections to select candidates for all political parties shall be held simultaneously. The time between primary and general elections shall not exceed four weeks and will include run off elections. Runoff elections shall commence one week after each election and shall last no longer than two weeks.

### **Section 4.** POLITICAL DONATIONS

Political contributions for elections may be requested and accepted by candidates or official representatives of candidates only during the four-month period prior to the day of the election.

Between elections, elected officials may not collect funds or benefits, directly or indirectly for any purposes, or by future promises, but are to focus on serving the best interests of the people.

## **Section 5.** WHO CAN DONATE TO ELECTION CAMPAIGNS

Political contributions may be made only by citizens of the United States and received only by a single campaign fund of qualified candidates and political parties.

Except for citizens, corporations, foreign governments, unions, persons from other countries, and all other entities, domestic or foreign are excluded from fund raising, donating or participating or advertising in political campaigns directly or indirectly.

These limitations apply to all federal, state and city elections in the United States.

All political donations must be solely in the monetary form of cash and all other forms of support including services or products are specifically prohibited.

## **Section 6.** CHOOSE THE BEST CANDIDATE

Donations from citizens may go to only one candidate in each election.

## **Section 7.** DOLLAR LIMITS PER CITIZEN

The combined total donations that each citizen may make to any election campaign shall not exceed $10,000 adjusted annually for changes in currency value.

Donations by citizens to political parties may be made only once annually, to only one political party, and may not exceed $10,000, adjusted annually for changes in currency value. All donations to a political party must go directly to its single national campaign general fund and may be used for publicizing the issues important to the party, conventions, and other expenses. Party donations, advertising, or other financial support to the campaign of any person seeking office is prohibited.

Political donations to any other persons or entities other than candidate's official campaign fund or political parties are prohibited.

Candidates losing a primary election of a political party shall turn over all unspent campaign monies remaining after their primary election to their political party, and those funds cannot be used to support any candidates in the general election.

Political contributions from lobbyists are specifically prohibited, and lobbyists are further forbidden from fundraising, providing of products or services, or direct or indirect support for any candidates or political party.

### **Section 8.** ELECTION REGULATIONS

Candidates may accept campaign donations from four months prior to the day of the election, but no earlier.

If the candidate fails to qualify all funds must be returned to the donors.

All forms of campaign advertising are permitted only during the six-week election periods and the two weeks of runoffs, and are specifically prohibited at all other times.

All candidates and political parties are responsible for the accuracy of the content of their respective campaigns.

Advertisements may only be accepted by all media from the official campaigns accompanied by the signature of the leader of the political party or the candidate. Campaign ads may be programmed only during election periods.

Use of party funds directly or indirectly for negative campaigning is strictly PROHIBITED.

### **Section 9.** CAMPAIGN EXPENDITURES

All monies donated for political purposes, regardless of source, shall be spent directly for and only for campaign purposes. From the date of qualifying to run for office, every candidate must publicly provide a weekly report of all donations as to the amount and source of all funds.

All candidates are personally responsible for all payments and shall certify that payment is within the capability of their campaign funds.

All candidates are prohibited from using their campaign donations directly or indirectly to support other candidates seeking office.

No later than thirty days after the election every candidate shall report to the general accounting office how all monies were received and spent, and any remaining balances or obligations.

Cash remaining after all general elections will become the property of the political party of that candidate.

### Section 10. MEDIA DEFINITIONS AND GUIDELINES

Campaign advertising is hereby defined to include all media, Internet, all forms of electronic communications, all written publications, and any other form of advertising. Campaign advertising or promotion in all forms may not be sold or accepted by any agency of media without the prior written approval of the candidate or political party placing the ad, and may be run only during the campaign period.

### Section 11. ENFORCEMENT

Violation of this amendment by political parties shall be punishable by a fine of no less than one million dollars for each violation.

Any candidate or person convicted of violating or subverting election law shall be subject to no less than a $100,000 fine and one-year mandatory imprisonment. Any offender who is an elected official or government employee shall also suffer permanent loss of all government benefits.

Any media executive that fails to comply with all constitutional election and campaign requirements shall be subject to a fine of no less than ten times the amount spent for improper advertising and no less than one-year imprisonment.

Lobbyists convicted for breach of any election law shall permanently lose their license, and be subject to no less than a $500,000 fine and mandatory one-year imprisonment.

### **Section 12.** THE ELECTORAL COLLEGE

Each state shall assign votes to the Electoral College between either of two methods. Electoral votes may be distributed in proportion to the statewide popular vote, or the majority vote in each congressional district, or a combination thereof. Candidates receiving less than 10% of the statewide popular vote shall have their electoral votes prorated among the other leading candidates.

### **Section 13.** GERRYMANDERING IS PROHIBITED

Realignment of the borders or districts within a state based on political party or voting preferences is prohibited. Districts for the election of all public offices shall be contiguous and coherent.

Most Americans have a limited appreciation of the sacrifice of time and effort running for office demands. Attending political meetings or watching speeches on TV give us only a brief glimpse of the total picture. The life of a candidate on the campaign trail is much different than what we perceive. We are unaware of the intense pressures that a candidate must endure in seeking elected office. This important information will help explain how the election system works, why it is dysfunctional, and why truly talented people refuse to run for office.

Candidates run for office for many reasons. There is the excitement, being on TV at the center of attention, and surely the idealistic intention of doing good if elected. Unfortunately the brutality of campaigning and the political reality once elected gradually change the candidate. Change is essential to survive the pressure and competition.

Presently our political campaigns are impossibly difficult! They are far too long, usually starting a year or more before qualifying, and it is a full time job at zero pay. The incumbent has all the advantages of voter recognition and political connections. The new candidate has to get to know the power players who control votes in their constituency and win them as friends. Money is critically needed, so the candidate must give hundreds of impressive speeches to attract the support of financially well-heeled people to finance his or her campaign. Millions have to be raised and it has to be done every day, day after day.

Simultaneously, the candidate must put together and pay for a politically skilled organization. Their staff has to develop the campaign schedule, provide transportation, obtain publicity, and make appointments with anyone and everyone who might help with votes or money. The candidate will also need qualified statisticians to run polls to find out their voting support level, how their opponents are doing, and what issues can improve their popularity. A campaign manager is needed to coordinate people and strategy. Each day candidates eat two to three breakfasts, lunches and dinners while giving so many speeches to multiple audiences that their voice is strained from begging for money, always graciously begging for money in exchange for promises.

During the last few months before the election the candidate will put in 12 to 14 hours daily, every day of the week. He or she will sleep in a different bed most nights and may possibly not go home to sleep in their own bed for a whole month or more. It is a closely timed schedule rushing from one event to the next in cars, buses, airplanes and taxis. It is physically and mentally exhausting.

Throughout the process the candidate and their staff must take great care to please the press and not make a single verbal gaffe that can kill their campaign. This is very stressful. Perhaps most frustrating is that the incumbent usually has better name recognition and money raising power.

Opponents will smear their reputation, and many people will insult them. Their health is put to the test by the grueling pace of the campaign. Perhaps the worst part is that there is no privacy, personal or intimate, for the candidate and their family. The press wants to know everything, and it is made public with minimal discretion and often inaccurately. After all this effort the candidate may only be lucky enough to get into a runoff, and campaigning starts all over again. <u>Is it any wonder that honest, successful and highly qualified people refuse to subject themselves to this ordeal?</u>

The outlook of human beings who go through this kind of ordeal gradually changes during the campaign. The early idealism blends into a different reality as one learns that politics is a tough competitive business.

Let's assume that there is good news on Election Day, and the candidate wins! As an official representative of the people, the oath of office is administered and he or she shows up for work to do good for the community. Reality sets in. The way legislation is passed is mostly wheeling and dealing. Votes must be cast for what others want in exchange for what is wanted for your constituency. You vote for it despite the fact much of it is against those fine ideals present when first deciding to run for office. Someone once compared legislation to making sausage, not a pretty picture.

Election reform in the United States is desperately needed. Congress has passed election laws over and over but none have any teeth. Supreme Court decisions perpetuates our long, expensive, and dysfunctional election process as part of free speech. Americans know changes are needed, but genuine election reform will never originate in Congress. Only Constitutional Amendments can streamline elections, prevent candidates from being "bought" by special interests, and refocus elected officials on serving the people.

Making real changes won't be easy because special interests are snugly in bed with candidates, and both will try to block genuine reform. Since candidates try to find loopholes to avoid election rules, successful reform must be all encompassing, precise, tough and practical. They will need popular support for passage, and be enforced with real penalties.

## <u>HERE'S WHAT TRUE ELECTION REFORM LOOKS LIKE</u>

Limit election campaigns to six weeks.

Control the time when donations may be solicited.

Define who can contribute, how much, and to whom.

Hold candidates personally responsible for their campaigns and campaign funds.

All candidates must prove they are American citizens.

Require proof of identity when voting.

Establish election regulations and procedures.

Establish penalties and enforcement.

Revise how the Electoral College elects Presidents.

Set Constitutional limits to gerrymandering.

The concepts proposed for this Amendment seek to introduce tough improvements with precise and binding language. Hopefully some of these ideas will be appealing to a Constitutional Convention.

The Founding Fathers left most of the qualifications to each individual state, and this has worked efficiently. One qualification we do need to impose on the states is the certainty that all federal candidates are indeed citizens of the United States.

## **Section 1.** CANDIDATE QUALIFICATIONS

All candidates seeking federal office must be American citizens.

### WHO CAN VOTE

Our laws make it clear that only registered citizens are authorized to vote. The question is, must voters provide proof of their identity when voting? The legal and ethical answer is YES.

We must provide identification to cash a check, board an airplane, get into a federal building, rent a video, get a driver's license or passport, and enter a country. Why not to vote? It is not profiling it is qualifying.

When identification is not required, elections are more easily rigged. Names can be fraudulently signed to a register to permit an illegal vote. In certain cities of the United States deceased people still on the rolls have been known to vote regularly. It's called ballot stuffing. Requiring positive identification is a solid step toward honest elections. It is not discrimination, and we should question the ethics of any politician who says identification is unnecessary.

Is voting a privilege or duty? Should voting be mandatory? I don't know, nor can I predict the outcome, were voting a legal requirement. Let's at least allow the states to make the decision, and see the outcome.

## **Section 2.** ONLY CITIZENS CAN VOTE

Only registered citizens of the United States may vote and must provide proof of identity when voting. States may choose to require that voting, subject to penalty, is mandatory.

### THE LENGTH OF ELECTIONS

Unofficially our elections start as soon as the last one is over. British elections are held for six weeks, and campaign advertising is limited to those six weeks. That system works beautifully! Shorter election times keep officials working longer for the people, limits the amount of money needed to run, levels the playing field between incumbents and challengers, and focus the population on who is the best candidate. It makes good sense. Six weeks for every election seems practical, but slightly longer or shorter intervals may be more appealing to a Constitutional Convention, but know this truth:

Six weeks is actually four months.

We would have six weeks for the primaries where each political party simultaneously selects its candidates. Requiring all political parties to hold their primaries simultaneously saves taxpayers money. After the primary there would be a four-week break that would include two weeks for necessary runoffs. Then we would have the actual election for six weeks followed by another four weeks including runoff elections. Six-week elections actually total sixteen weeks or about four months, and that is plenty! The biggest advantage is that less money is needed and that is part of the formula to elect politicians who are truly independent and can serve the people.

## **Section 3.** SIX-WEEK PRIMARIES AND ELECTIONS

All primary and general elections shall be for no more than six weeks. Primary elections to select candidates for all political parties shall be held simultaneously. The time between primary and general elections shall not exceed four weeks and will include run off elections. Runoff elections shall commence one week after each election and shall last no longer than two weeks.

### **CAMPAIGN DONATIONS**

The most demeaning part of being a politician is seeking big money and/or benefits to get elected and thus obligate your self to deliver special benefits ultimately at taxpayer expense. Wal-Mart does not permit its buyers to accept anything, not even a cup of coffee from suppliers. That assures that the buyer is independent and can make objective decisions on what to buy. Don't we want the same ethics and independence for our elected officials?

Presently, elected officials and prospective candidates start collecting campaign funds years in advance of elections. It distracts them from their public responsibilities and invites financially powerful interests to gain excessive influence.

We start by limiting <u>when</u> donations may be offered and accepted by elected officials so they stay focused on their jobs. Money can only be offered and accepted during the four months preceding the Election Day. Many politicians collect donations year around for other than election purposes. These monies and gifts that fall <u>outside</u> of all legal regulations are blatant conflicts of interest and must be prohibited.

## **Section 4.** POLITICAL DONATIONS

Political contributions for elections may be requested and accepted by candidates or official representatives of candidates only during the four-month period prior to the day of the election.

Between elections, elected officials may not collect funds or benefits, directly or indirectly for any purposes, or by future promises, but are to focus on serving the best interests of the people.

## WHO MAY DONATE CAMPAIGN MONEY?

Political contributions and other benefits are at the heart of government corruption. Because big money compromises elected officials, the **key questions are WHO should be permitted to donate to election campaigns, and HOW MUCH?**

Citizens have the right to vote, and those who vote decide elections. Since the government is supposed to serve the citizens, why should entities other than citizens be permitted to donate any money at all?

Corporations don't vote, so why should they be permitted to donate money? PACs and Unions don't vote, so why should they be permitted to donate money? These entities are legal entities, they do not alive, citizens are people and the government serves the people.

Foreign governments, aliens, and other political entities don't vote either, so why should they be permitted to donate money? The motives of contributors, other than voters, clearly represent special or conflicting interests different from those of the people and our nation at large.

Good government serves its citizens and only citizens should be permitted the choice of making political donations.

**To clean up elections ONLY citizens should be permitted to make campaign donations**! This should be a policy for all elections, federal, state and city. To prevent alternate kinds of support, donations should be limited ONLY to CASH. No other forms such as free rent, food, and whiskey should be permitted.

## **Section 5.** WHO MAY DONATE TO ELECTION CAMPAIGNS

Political contributions may be made only by citizens of the United States and received only by a single campaign fund of qualified candidates and political parties.

Except for citizens, corporations, foreign governments, unions, persons from other countries, and all other entities, domestic or foreign are excluded from fund raising, donating or participating or advertising in political campaigns directly or indirectly.

These limitations apply to all federal, state and city elections in the United States.

All political donations must be solely in the monetary form of cash and all other forms of support including services or products are specifically prohibited.

### HOW MANY DOLLARS?

Next we must determine the maximum amount of money any one citizen can contribute to any one candidate and political party. The wealthy must not be permitted to buy sufficient influence to put their interests ahead of the nation. The amounts and names of all contributors must be transparent to the public and reported promptly each week during the election.

In the 2008 Presidential election, the Republican candidate spent over $300 million, and the Democratic candidate over $700 million.

For the 2012 Presidential election, the August 13th edition of *Time* estimated that Romney would spend $600 million and combined with other PAC support the total would reach $1.35 billion. President Obama is estimated to have spent $800 million with the total Democratic package at about $1.16 billion.

The total of all monies spent for the 2012 federal elections by all candidates is estimated to have approached six billion dollars!

In the last election, single individuals repeatedly gave multiple donations exceeding one million dollars as the campaign proceeded. Can there be any doubt that that kind of money compromises candidates? The truth is that our elections are early negotiations for government benefits. Those millions in donations create obligations that cost the taxpayers billions for special interests.

Specific donation limits per person are essential, with tough punishments enforced even after elections for breach of law.

We can safely assume that tight limits on the amount of money will cause tremendous objections by elected officials, lobbyists and special interests. But with short six-week elections, many small donations from interested citizens will be more than sufficient to finance election expenses including television spots. This is especially true if advertising can only be run during the six weeks. Since these rules will apply to all candidates, they are quite equitable. Let the best candidate win.

It is very important that a Constitutional Convention recommend an Amendment that only citizens can donate and with a specific dollar limit that a citizen can donate to any one candidate or political party. Otherwise incumbents may legislate larger amounts restoring excessive influence to the wealthy. Donation limits of up to $10,000 are unlikely to compromise candidates once the election is over.

Lobbyists should be kept totally out of elections. The farm bill of 2013 is an example of how much money in involved. The Center for Responsive Politics, which tracks political spending, reported that lobbyists on the Senate bill spent over $150 million. The money came from at least 350 companies and organizations including Monsanto, PepsiCo, and Dean Foods. Lobbyists are needed for their essential role to inform and educate elected officials <u>when the elections are over</u>. When lobbyists provide money or services for politicians it is outright bribery and must be prohibited.

Most politicians exhaust their campaign treasury. On the rare occasion where money is left over it should not permitted for use as a slush fund.

### **Section 6.** <u>DOLLAR LIMITS PER CITIZEN</u>

The combined total donations that each citizen may make to any election campaign shall not exceed $10,000 adjusted annually for changes in currency value.

Donations by citizens to political parties may be made only once annually, to only one political party, and may not exceed $10,000, adjusted annually for changes in currency value. All donations to a political party must go directly to its single national campaign general fund and may be used for publicizing the issues important to the party, conventions, and other expenses. Party donations, advertising, or other financial support to the campaign of any person seeking office is prohibited.

Political donations to any other persons or entities other than candidate's official campaign fund or political parties are prohibited.

Candidates losing a primary election of a political party shall turn over all unspent campaign monies remaining after their primary election to their political party, and those funds cannot be used to support any candidates in the general election.

Political contributions from lobbyists are specifically prohibited, and lobbyists are further forbidden from fundraising, providing of products or services, or direct or indirect support for any candidates or political party.

## CHOOSING THE BEST CANDIDATE

**Isn't the objective of every election to select the *best* candidate?** Those who choose to support more than one candidate for the same office surely have a different motivation than electing the best candidate. Is that motive good for our country?

Presently some citizens give donations to <u>many</u> candidates in the <u>same election</u>. It is blatant bribery. Let's limit donations by individuals to only one candidate in each election.

## **Section 7.** <u>CHOOSE THE BEST CANDIDATE</u>
Donations from citizens may go to only one candidate in each election.

### CANDIDATES ARE RESPONSIBLE FOR THEIR ELECTION CAMPAIGN

Recognizing that television and many other media businesses earn large profits from the present system that spends billions, it is probable that they will oppose these reforms. Hopefully they will appreciate that these changes are in their best interest and for the benefit of our nation and future generations.

The only campaigns in any race for political office should be those of the candidates themselves. Candidates must have the character to be responsible for how every penny of their campaign money is spent. Advertising of all kinds must be limited solely to money personally authorized by the candidates and no one else. Campaign advertising should be permitted only during the election period.

To enforce these rules, all media should be legally limited to accepting political advertisements only from candidates and political parties, and running the ads only during the election period. This stops unethical groups from raising money for negative advertising, and the making of false, slanderous, and cruel claims just before the election.

### Section 8. ELECTION REGULATIONS

Candidates may accept campaign donations from four months prior to the day of the election, but no earlier.

If the candidate fails to qualify all funds must be returned to the donors.

All forms of campaign advertising are permitted only during the six-week election periods and the two weeks of runoffs, and are specifically prohibited at all other times.

All candidates and political parties are responsible for the accuracy of the content of their respective campaigns.

Advertisements may only be accepted by all media from the official campaigns accompanied by the signature of the leader of the political party or the candidate. Campaign ads may be programmed only during election periods.

Use of party funds directly or indirectly for negative campaigning is strictly PROHIBITED.

### Section 9. CAMPAIGN EXPENDITURES

All monies donated for political purposes, regardless of source, shall be spent directly for and only for campaign purposes. From the date of qualifying to run for office, every candidate must publicly provide a weekly report of all donations as to the amount and source of all funds.

All candidates are personally responsible for all payments and shall certify that payment is within the capability of their campaign funds.

All candidates are prohibited from using their campaign donations directly or indirectly to support other candidates seeking office.

No later than thirty days after the election every candidate shall report to the general accounting office how all monies were received and spent, and any remaining balances or obligations.

Cash remaining after all general elections will become the property of the political party of that candidate.

## **Section 10.** MEDIA DEFINITIONS AND GUIDELINES

Campaign advertising is hereby defined to include all media, Internet, all forms of electronic communications, all written publications, and any other form of advertising. Campaign advertising or promotion in all forms may not be sold or accepted by any agency of media without the prior written approval of the candidate or political party placing the ad, and may be run only during the campaign period.

Enforcement of Constitutional Election Law is a challenge. Much depends on the ethics of those in office, specifically the President, and the Attorney General. Yet punishment is essential for credibility. The press should inform the people when a breach of law has occurred, and people can judge the guilt of candidates that breach the Constitution. Yet enforced punishment is the only way to be sure laws are followed.

## **Section 11.** ENFORCEMENT

Violation of this amendment by political parties shall be punishable by a fine of no less than one million dollars for each violation.

Any candidate or person convicted of violating or subverting election law shall be subject to no less than a $100,000 fine and one-year mandatory imprisonment. Any offender who is an elected official or government employee shall also suffer permanent loss of all government benefits.

Any media executive that fails to comply with all constitutional election and campaign requirements shall be subject to a fine of no less than ten times the amount spent for improper advertising and no less than one-year imprisonment.

Lobbyists convicted for breach of any election law shall permanently lose their license, and be subject to no less than a $500,000 fine and mandatory one-year imprisonment.

## THE ELECTORAL COLLEGE

There is very justified concern about how the Electoral College operates because of the "block" vote rule. The Constitution says that, whoever wins the majority of the popular vote in each state receives ALL of that state's Electoral College votes. This has very adversely affected Presidential elections.

In the 2012 election both Presidential candidates focused their campaigns on nine large states that had sufficient <u>electoral</u> votes to win the Presidency. *That effectively disenfranchised the remaining 41 states.* Surely that is not a national Presidential election.

An alternative, by direct popular vote by disbanding the Electoral College has serious drawbacks. A President elected by only a few votes might not be considered to have a solid mandate. Worse still is the danger that voting disputes would make it impossible to promptly determine who has been elected President. That decision could be delayed by recounts and litigation, dangerously leaving that office empty for weeks or months.

An excellent compromise that has already proven both practical and precise has been adopted by two states. Maine and Nebraska use the "congressional district method," selecting one elector within each congressional district by popular vote and selecting the remaining electors by a statewide popular vote.

This compromise makes the election of our President a truly national election. It assures that all the people, in all the states, participate in electing the President, but it too has a potential weakness.

A small third political party candidate could conceivably collect sufficient electoral votes to cause a bargaining event for the election of President. To avoid this predicament, very small third parties must be prohibited from receiving electoral votes. The Amendment proposed below assures that every state in the nations is involved in the election of President of the United States of America.

## **Section 12.** THE ELECTORAL COLLEGE

Each state shall assign votes to the Electoral College between either of two methods. Electoral votes may be distributed in proportion to the statewide popular vote, or the majority vote in each congressional district, or a combination thereof. Candidates receiving less than 10% of the statewide popular vote shall have their electoral votes prorated among the other leading candidates.

There is a political requirement of our Constitution that the number of Representative in the House be redistributed after every census based on how our population has grown and relocated. This redistribution created a political technique called gerrymandering. The party in power in each state draws voting district lines that increases the certainty their party's candidates will be elected. This is a distortion not intended by the Constitution.

## **Section 12.** GERRYMANDERING IS PROHIBITED

Realignment of the borders or districts within a state based on political party or voting preferences is prohibited. Districts for the election of all public offices shall be contiguous and coherent.

## Chapter Three

# ETHICS AND PERFORMANCE

At the time our Constitution was written, royal families held supreme authority in Europe. Kings and Queens had the power of life and death. Our Founding Fathers were convinced that the elitism of royalty was abusive to the people and they would have none of it. Believing that all men should share equal privileges and opportunities, they created the concept of the "free man" and defined freedom as "the inalienable right to life, liberty, and the pursuit of happiness." Inherent in this concept is the *absence of an elite power group*.

Our elected officials have passed laws providing to themselves privileges and benefits well beyond those guaranteed to U.S. citizens. They receive medical care and other benefits that are far more generous than citizens, and pay less than citizens. They burden the citizens with taxes and regulations while exempting themselves. Until recently, they did "inside trading" that is criminal for citizens.

Our "professional politicians" have become the *elite* our Founding Fathers feared! Benefit limits for elected officials need to be delineated in the Constitution, not determined by and for themselves. The following Amendments enforce several concepts designed to achieve the highest standards of ethics of behavior for persons elected, appointed or employed in public service.

## Section 1. NO ELITISM

The twenty-seventh article of Amendment to the Constitution of the United States is hereby repealed. Congress shall not enact laws or statutes that apply to the citizens of the United States that do not apply equally to Congress and the President; and, Congress shall make no laws or statutes that apply to Congress and the President that do not apply equally to all citizens of the United States. Laws previously enacted inconsistent with this amendment, regardless of when passed, shall become null and void retroactively when this amendment is ratified.

## Section 2. PAY AND BENEFITS

The President shall earn an annual salary of ten million dollars with an annual million-dollar expense account. Senators shall earn an annual salary of four million dollars with a four hundred thousand dollar annual expense account, and Representatives shall earn an annual salary of one million dollars with an annual expense account of two hundred thousand dollars. Retirement benefits for both salary and expense accounts shall be half of the above amounts. These values shall be adjusted annually based on the change in the value of the dollar. All other benefits shall be the same as those of the citizens.

## **Section 3.** EXECUTIVE ORDERS AND NOMINATIONS

All executive orders signed and issued by the president are to be promptly reported to the Senate and House of Representatives, and shall not be implemented for thirty days. If, during that period, a majority of the House of Representatives or Senate may by vote while in session, or electronically when not in session, submit that executive order to the Supreme Court for a ruling as to its Constitutionality. The Supreme Court shall make a prompt ruling on all such challenges and the executive order shall not be implemented until the court rules. During a declared war the thirty-day delay may be waived at the President's option but Congress's right to challenge its Constitutionality shall not be abridged.

The President may nominate appointments only when the Senate is in session, but not during the thirty days before adjourning. If within thirty days the senate does not disapprove Presidential nominees, they shall be considered approved.

## **Section 4.** ETHICS AND GIFTS

Elected officials, appointed officials, all civil service employees, civilian employees of the government, and their immediate family shall not request, accept, or receive personal donations, gifts, remunerations or any other benefits directly or indirectly while in government employ or promises of future benefits. If prosecuted for any civil or criminal offense in breach of their public trust, they shall not receive financial support from the government in their defense.

If convicted of any felony offense occurring while in government service, they and their family shall permanently lose their salary, retirement, medical care and all other government benefits, and none shall be reinstated, nor may they again serve the government in any capacity, nor may the President pardon them for this breach of public trust.

## **Section 5.** POLITICAL NEUTRALITY

All employees of the federal government, except for voting, are prohibited from actively participating in politics in any manner including donating or raising money, working in election campaigns, being active in political parties, and providing private or public assistance of any kind to candidates or political parties. Breach of this amendment is punishable by discharge from employment with permanent loss of all benefits.

### Section 6. PERFORMANCE REQUIREMENTS
Government employees may be discharged by order of the executive department for failure to consistently perform their responsibilities with the highest standard of excellence, a cooperative attitude, and prompt attendance to work.

### Section 7. CLARITY OF LEGISLATION
All laws shall be written in easily understood English where there is no doubt as to the meaning, intention, and expected consequences.

### Section 8. CONFLICTS OF INTEREST
All elected or appointed employees of the federal government are prohibited from employment as a lobbyist for a period of four years after separation from government service, nor may they accept any future commitment of employment while in government service, nor while in office may any immediate family member of an elected official be employed as a lobbyist.

### Section 9. PROHIBIT FOREIGN LOBBYING
Elected officials, appointed officials, and government employees may not accept campaign

funds, gifts, or benefits of any kind from foreign citizens, other governments, or representatives of foreign interests subject to a fine of no less than $500,000, two years imprisonment, and permanent loss of all government benefits.

Politicians, appointed officials, and government employees should work and receive pay commensurate to the value of their work. There should be no privileged class in America.

## **Section 1.** NO ELITISM

The twenty-seventh article of Amendment to the Constitution of the United States is hereby repealed. Congress shall not enact laws or statutes that apply to the citizens of the United States that do not apply equally to Congress and the President; and, Congress shall make no laws or statutes that apply to Congress and the President that do not apply equally to all citizens of the United States. Laws previously enacted inconsistent with this amendment, regardless of when passed, shall become null and void retroactively when this amendment is ratified.

The above Amendment leaves unanswered the question of how much our elected officials shall be paid. We need to designate the pay and benefits of elected officials. While public service is a heady ego-lifting experience, the pay should be commensurate with the responsibilities. The President administers the largest budget in the world, and Congress passes an annual budget in the trillions of dollars every year. That is indeed a big responsibility. Elected officials also sacrifice much of their privacy, family time, and often work extraordinary hours. Shouldn't pay and benefits be specific and generous to attract the best candidates?

Isn't it better to provide generously and then set high standards of ethics with severe punishments for breach of any public trust? High pay with an expense account helps reduce vulnerability to bribery and also encourages highly qualified people earning big incomes to run for office. Long-term retirement benefits further assure independence while in office. It is best if this is done at the Constitutional level with inflation adjustments.

## **Section 2.** PAY AND BENEFITS

The President shall earn an annual salary of ten million dollars with an annual million-dollar expense account. Senators shall earn an annual salary of four million dollars with a four hundred thousand dollar annual expense account, and Representatives shall earn an annual salary of one million dollars with an annual expense account of two hundred thousand dollars. Retirement benefits for both salary and expense accounts shall be half of the above amounts. These values shall be adjusted annually based on the change in the value of the dollar. All other benefits shall be the same as those of the citizens.

Over time, Presidents have pushed to increase the power of the executive branch beyond the limits defined in the Constitution. This has been done through the use of *executive orders*. On the other hand, solely for political reasons, the Senate has deliberately withheld approving nominees to serve the executive or judicial branches. In exchange the President has made appointments when Congress is out of session. To keep power properly balanced between the executive and legislative branches, the following method of congressional oversight of executive orders and Presidential appointments is suggested.

## **Section 3.** EXECUTIVE ORDERS AND NOMINATIONS

All executive orders signed and issued by the president are to be promptly reported to the Senate and House of Representatives, and shall not be implemented for thirty days. If, during that period, a majority of the House of Representatives or Senate may by vote while in session, or electronically when not in session, submit that executive order to the Supreme Court for a ruling as to its Constitutionality. The Supreme Court shall make a prompt ruling on all such challenges and the executive order shall not be implemented until the court rules. During a declared war the thirty-day delay may be waived at the President's option but Congress's right to challenge its Constitutionality shall not be abridged.

The President may nominate appointments only when the Senate is in session, but not during the thirty days before adjourning. If within thirty days the senate does not disapprove Presidential nominees, they shall be considered approved.

Every government employees has a *"public trust."* Elected officials, those serving by appointment, and all other personnel have that responsibility. Their sacred public trust is to maintain the highest standard of ethics in the performance of their duties. Today, there is little downside for those who violate that sacred trust. Our government pays their legal defense, and if convicted and sent to jail, their salary and benefits usually continue uninterrupted.

Bribery is not discussed in our Constitution, as the Founding Fathers felt Congress would pass appropriate laws and enforce them. Congress has failed to enforce ethical standards within its own membership, much less throughout the government bureaucracy. It is clear that stronger guidelines need to be established in the Constitution.

Since Congress will not do it, a Constitutional Amendment is needed.

## **Section 4.** ETHICS AND GIFTS

Elected officials, appointed officials, all civil service employees, civilian employees of the government, and their immediate family shall not request, accept, or receive personal donations, gifts, remunerations or any other benefits directly or indirectly while in government employ or promises of future benefits. If prosecuted for any civil or criminal offense in breach of their public trust, they shall not receive financial support from the government in their defense.

If convicted of any felony offense occurring while in government service, they and their family shall permanently lose their salary, retirement, medical care and all other government benefits, and none shall be reinstated, nor may they again serve the government in any capacity, nor may the President pardon them for this breach of public trust.

The Founding Fathers prohibited government employees and the military from voting. They believed that because they are government employees it would be a conflict of interest. Considering the millions of government employees today, this conflict of interest has become real. Many government employees are unionized wielding such significant political power that politicians have an incentive to cater to them and increase the size of government bureaucracies to help get reelected.

It seems appropriate to limit all government employees from political activity. Since our politicians will never correct this situation, Constitutional change is necessary.

## **Section 5.** POLITICAL NEUTRALITY

All employees of the federal government except for voting, are prohibited from actively participating in politics in any manner including donating or raising money, working in election campaigns, being active in political parties, and providing private or public assistance of any kind to candidates or political parties. Breach of this amendment is punishable by discharge from employment with permanent loss of all benefits.

In years past, when elections changed the political party in power, patronage became abusive. Qualified public employees were fired and replaced with friends of the newly elected officials. Civil Service was enacted to protect public employees from politics. Now union membership adds additional protection. The combination of civil service and union protection makes government employees almost immune from justified discipline, discharge for poor performance, or incompetence.

Surely we all agree that government employees should maintain a positive and friendly attitude, perform their duties with a high standard of excellence, and follow work rules. Civil Service/union employees should be as competitive and competent as their counterparts in the private sector.

### **Section 6.** PERFORMANCE REQUIREMENTS
Government employees may be discharged by order of the executive department for failure to consistently perform their responsibilities with the highest standard of excellence, a cooperative attitude, and prompt attendance to work.

When writing laws, to avoid embarrassment, Congress often uses language designed to conceal benefits secretly granted to special interests. It would be unpleasant if the truth became public. Legislation should be clear, understandable, and have no hidden meanings.

### **Section 7.** LEGISLATIVE TRANSPARENCY
All laws shall be written in easily understood English where there is no doubt as to the meaning, intention, and expected consequences.

If while serving in office, elected officials agree to become a lobbyist or agree to accept other employment in the future after their term of office is complete, they immediately compromise their office. Furthermore, if any member of their family is an active lobbyist while they are in office, again they are compromised. As concerned citizens we must demand the highest standard of ethics from all public servants. Elected officials cannot properly serve the people with any conflicts of interest.

## **Section 8.** CONFLICTS OF INTEREST

All elected or appointed employees of the federal government are prohibited from employment as a lobbyist for a period of four years after separation from government service, nor may they accept any future commitment of employment while in government service, nor while in office may any immediate family member of an elected official be employed as a lobbyist.

Currently foreign interests lobby and provide donations and benefits to candidates seeking office, elected officials, appointees, and government employees. That is NOT in the best interest of our nation.

## **Section 9.** PROHIBIT FOREIGN LOBBYING

Elected officials, appointed officials, and government employees may not accept campaign funds, gifts, or benefits of any kind from foreign citizens, other governments, or representatives of foreign interests subject to a fine of no less than $500,000, two years imprisonment, and permanent loss of all government benefits.

## Chapter Four

# A RESPONSIBLE AND TRUTHFUL PRESS

None of these changes are intended to alter First Amendment rights of our free press.

## Section 1. PRIVACY

The privacy of all citizens may not be invaded including personal health, intimacy, finances or any other family information. This information may not be made public without that individual's prior written consent or that of their heirs.

## Section 2. TRUTH

The responsibility of a free press, all media and businesses engaged in communications, all gatherers of information, reporters, editors, producers, and publishers is to faithfully report the best, most accurate and reliable version of the truth, without minimization or exaggeration.

## **Section 3.** PENALTIES

Any reporting of untruths or abuse of citizens' privacy is punishable with financial penalties sufficient to compensate the damaged parties, but such penalties shall not be financially crippling to a free press.

## **Section 4.** MEDIA INDEPENDENCE

The ownership, board of directors, and executives of businesses engaged in communications and all media shall confine their business solely to that industry. None may do business directly or indirectly with the federal government, nor may any single business or combination thereof represent more than 20% of the market share.

The American Press is possibly the freest and most informative of any in the world, and we should be proud of our TV, radio, newspapers and other forms of communication.

It is not my intention to reduce the freedom of our press in any way. Reporting news and information is actually a highly skilled profession, and it is my hope that the press will embrace these proposed Amendments, recognizing that they will further enhance the respect for their profession.

These Amendments seek to raise the ethical standards and quality of information reported to the people. A free, responsible, and truthful press is essential to an informed electorate. Let me go one step further, a misinformed public may well elect a government that is oppressive, even destructive to freedom.

A brief history will demonstrate why **responsibility** is so important to a truly professional free press. Let's start by addressing the significance that must be placed on personal privacy and the basic respect for people. Just because the press has information, responsible judgment should be used in deciding if the information is publicized. That judgment tells a lot about the true quality of those reporting information.

When privacy is not **respected** the consequences are emotionally painful and financially destructive to citizens, businesses, and definitely to our country. Invasion of privacy is not only disruptive to our personal freedom and safety, but to elections and the quality of our government. Let me demonstrate with some actual situations where the press was responsible for great good and serious harm.

Princess Diana would probably be alive if her privacy needs had been respected by the paparazzi.

Some of our great Presidents would never have been elected if our press had not disciplined itself ethically by respecting their privacy. George Washington and Thomas Jefferson had mistresses. Benjamin Franklin seduced women wherever he went and stayed away from home for years. Abraham Lincoln had a nervous breakdown and yet literally saved our nation during one of the most stressful periods in our history. In those days surely the press knew about those flaws, yet this information turns up only in history books. Had the press damaged the reputations of those men, might it have deprived us of leadership that was essential to the founding of our nation?

Franklin Roosevelt was rumored to have a mistress visit with him in the White House. He was also paralyzed from polio and needed a wheelchair and crutches. Because of **respect for privacy**, the press never showed him in a wheelchair or crutches. Only after his death were Americans visibly made aware of his infirmity. Today if Roosevelt ran for office the TV cameras might zoom in on the shining spokes of his wheelchair possibly preventing him from being elected. Yet he was one of our most capable, popular, and successful Presidents guiding us out of the Great Depression and to victory in World War II.

Politicians are people with weaknesses just like the rest of us.

Shouldn't we select leaders for their character, experience, and intellect, not for their frailties and personal lives?

It takes a tough experienced leader to be President. The President has to deal with leaders of other nations who are shrewd and often ruthless. Most political leaders have high libidos, and at least some bad habits. Does our press highlight weaknesses rather than focusing on strengths and capabilities? By destroying a candidate's reputation through emphasizing human frailties, they may deprive us of potentially great leadership. America clearly needs strong competent leadership with the political savvy to get elected and the wisdom to get good things done.

That is why election reforms need to curtail negative advertising. We elect leaders hopefully for the good they may be capable of achieving and the American people are generally forgiving of human frailty.

All of us deserve the protection of personal privacy. All of us have imperfections, make mistakes, and have intimate parts to our lives that should remain private. We are entitled to Constitutional protection of our privacy unless we consent otherwise in writing.

## **Section 1.** PRIVACY

The privacy of all citizens may not be invaded including personal health, intimacy, finances or any other family information. This information may not be made public without that individual's prior written consent or that of their heirs.

Most sincerely, our press needs to address its own ethics in reporting the truth. Americans need the best and most accurate version of the truth if we are to remain a free people. Wrong information means wrong decisions. Our press has evolved so slowly in its drift away from keeping truth on the highest pedestal that it doesn't even realize what has happened.

In the 1800's newspapers and magazines were the main sources of information for citizens. Editors and publishers had pride in delivering truth and trusting the citizens to be capable of making their own decisions.

Opinions were described as "editorials" and had double columns. The column on the **"left"** proposed *change*. The column on the **"right"** supported the *status quo*. Editors would pick two reporters to do the research for each point of view. One was assigned the pro position and one to the con. Each reporter sought to provide only the facts and probable consequences. Informed with both views, citizens proved perfectly capable of making their own independent decisions. It also built good reporting skills.

Because written words are permanent, poor reporting and errors were embarrassing. The press avoided exaggeration and inaccuracy. Being precisely truthful was professional.

Today electronic information on television, radio, and the Internet quickly disappears. It is more difficult to affix responsibility when truth is blurred. Most importantly, electronic media have generated a new kind of competitive pressure more intense than the circulation of printed newspapers. Attracting viewers and obtaining high ratings is essential to success.

Sponsors pay the bills, and pay dearly for shows with higher ratings. News is no longer information; it has become *entertainment*. News and weather programs are called "shows" and their dramatic value has gradually become critical to survival, blurring the importance of accuracy in the content.

Our press also seems to believe that it needs to influence public opinion rather than inform. Too often the political outlook of the production, editorial or reporting staff color the news in the direction that they think is most correct. That is not a right of a free press. The liberal press in the East and West has helped elect Democrats. The conservative press in the South and Midwest has helped elect Republicans. Just the facts would be better.

Reporting of semi-truths, innuendoes, or out-of-context information can harm any person, business, and even a nation. What happened to a truly *objective press* that assumes their job is to present all the facts, fully inform the public, and let the American people make their own decisions?

Some Americans recognize that to capture public interest the news is deliberately dramatized. Unfortunately, most Americans believe and trust the press and they get misled when truth gets trampled. Americans historically respect truth. George Washington "could not tell a lie." Abraham Lincoln was called "honest Abe" because his word of honor was so respected.

Problem-solving solutions seldom appear because they are not exciting enough for viewers, but they could be. Instead, bad news is emphasized, often directed at a person, industry, and even our country. Simply put, our free press has been unwittingly changed by the pressures of electronic reporting and the need for high viewership ratings. Accuracy in reporting facts in an unbiased objective manner, once the pride of our press, needs to be restored.

What is a reasonable expectation?

The truly professional press should provide ***the best, most precise version of the truth!*** That is an essential responsibility of a *free* press. We do not want to curtail the freedom of our press, but we do need to make sure it is <u>truthful.</u> Rather than limit the power of the press, let's set them a definition of excellence and put it into the Constitution.

## <u>Section 2.</u> TRUTH

The responsibility of a free press, all media and businesses engaged in communications, all gatherers of information, reporters, editors, producers, and publishers is to faithfully report the best, most accurate and reliable version of the truth, without minimization or exaggeration.

We have addressed responsibility and truth, now we come to enforcement. It is preferable for Congress to <u>legislate</u> enforcement, but to avoid criticism for omission, here is an Amendment that empowers citizens while protecting our free press.

## <u>Section 3.</u> PENALTIES

Any reporting of untruths or abuse of citizens' privacy is punishable with financial penalties sufficient to compensate the damaged parties, but such penalties shall not be financially crippling to a free press.

Is our press truly free and independent? The issue is in doubt! <u>Today the financial control of our press is concentrated in a few giant conglomerates. Because</u>

these huge businesses have our government as a big customer, **conflicts of interest exist**.

Editors, producers, and reporters may have accepted "self-censoring guidelines" as good reporting, but is it? Are they aware that upper management may have instituted those guidelines designed to limit the reporting of information that may offend or embarrass important politicians?

Constant mergers occur in the communication industry. Here are some of the relationships and con-solidation of power in the communication industry existent at the time of publication.

General Electric, a major government military contractor, owns 20% of NBC Universal, the majority of which is now owned by Comcast the largest cable provider. NBC Universal also owns a major television network (NBC Television), many television stations, major cable news channels and Internet information providers. Comcast is buying out Time Warner Cable to further con-solidate the industry. Warren Buffet and George Soros are major investors in NBC Universal and have given big financial donations to President Obama. Disney owns ABC Television Network and several cable services. Time-Warner owns CNN, HBO and the Turner cable channels. These giant conglomerates owning communication businesses also have the government as a very large customer in other divisions of their companies. They also receive many millions for political advertising.

They cannot afford to offend elected officials because it might lose gigantic government contracts or offend the FCC (Federal Communications Commission). This small clique of communication ownership concentrates control of what we see, hear, and read into too few companies. Financial necessity to avoid offending government officials may influence our press to omit, slant, or manipulate information that affects public opinion to the advantage of special interests.

There should be <u>no doubt</u> that our press is <u>independent</u>. Those employed in the industry should want it independent, and they deserve that freedom. We need to separate the ownership and control of our communication businesses from all government connections to assure independence.

This is not difficult. Spinning off communication firms from their parent conglomerates, electing independent boards of directors, and diversifying ownership can peacefully end these potential conflicts. Our press must always be both free and INDEPENDENT.

## **Section 4.** MEDIA INDEPENDENCE

The ownership, board of directors, and executives of businesses engaged in communications and all media shall confine their business solely to that industry. None may do business directly or indirectly with the federal government, nor may any single business or combination thereof represent more than 20% of the market share.

# Chapter Five

# TORT AND LEGAL REFORMS

### Section 1. REDUCE LITIGATION
The losing party in all litigation shall pay all of the winner's reasonable legal expenses, and if unable to pay, then the losing litigant's attorney(s) shall be responsible for said payment.

### Section 2. PROMPT JUSTICE
Judges are required to expedite all cases in an appropriate manner. Defendants, plaintiffs, and judges shall each have the right to only one continuance so that trials shall not be unduly delayed.

### Section 3. FAIRNESS
Punitive damages shall be paid to the federal, state, or city government as appropriate, not to the defendant.

## **Section 4.** LEGAL ETHICS

During trials, if attorneys make statements not relevant to the specific case, deliberately distort evidence, or include information unrelated to the trial, such that the consequences tend to obfuscate the truth, or exaggerate, minimize, or distort facts sufficient to cause a mistrial, the judge may fine or suspend the attorney from the practice of law for up to one year.

## **Section 5.** SPEEDING CONSTITUTIONAL RULINGS

All Constitutional challenges as to law or court rulings shall proceed directly to the appellate courts where favorable decisions must be unanimous else the law or judgment is unconstitutional, and a favorable majority of six judges of the Supreme Court is required to rule that a law or lower court decision is constitutional else the law is unconstitutional.

Twenty-five members of the Congress may submit a law or judgment directly to the Supreme Court for a prompt ruling as to its constitutionality.

## **Section 6.** PREVENTING COURT ORDERED LEGISLATION

Federal courts are prohibited from ordering any remedy not already available under federal law.

## Section 7. FEDERAL JUDGES

The President shall nominate federal judges, a majority of the Senate shall recommend them for approval, and a majority of the governors of the states shall confirm them, the governors having forty-five days after Senate approval to reject the nomination in writing to the President or the nominee shall be deemed approved.

Federal judges must retire at age eighty.

## Section 8. OFFICIAL LANGUAGE

The official language of the United States is English.

Lawyers protect our freedoms. A good lawyer is like a knight on a white horse protecting our interests. Every citizen has the right to correct an injustice by filing a lawsuit in regards to equity, property, ownership, personal privacy or other injustice. We can even sue our government and win. The Constitution also provides that justice shall be speedy.

In recent decades changes in legal practices have altered the way our courts dispense justice. Speedy and cost-efficient trials have virtually disappeared. Federal, state and city courts are jammed with litigation. Suits continue for two to five years and in some cases for decades. Justice needs Constitutional repair.

In the past the legal profession was highly respected. Attorneys waited in their offices for clients to arrive, charges reflected the value of the legal work done, and results were prompt. That changed when lawyers started advertising their services. TV ads entice the public with glib promises suggesting they will receive exorbitant amounts of money for all kinds of damages assuring them that they are victims.

If a drinker has an automobile collision while drunk, is it the driver's fault? No, say the lawyers, it is the fault of the bartender who served him too many drinks. Bartenders must monitor how much alcohol their clients have consumed and stop serving them, lest they do something wrong while inebriated.

The list of the amazing reasons lawyers file suits would make a book in itself. Outrageous litigation has helped build a psychology where people are no longer responsible for their own decisions, actions and the outcomes.

### Frivolous litigation is a big expense for all Americans.

No one objects to lawyers making a good living, but they have turned the law into a moneymaking machine with class actions, liability suits, and all kinds of other claims to generate huge fees. Judgments in millions and even billions of dollars have drastically increased the cost of liability insurance for doctors, hospitals, households, and auto insurance for citizens. The cost of liability insurance is estimated to account for 10% - 16% of our nation's medical expenses.

A huge number of suits without merit are filed because there is no downside. Attorneys receive settlement money from insurance companies to drop worthless suits because a trial would cost much more. Litigation to prove that a defendant is innocent is so expensive that over 90% of suits are settled at the very last minute on the "courthouse steps." Frivolous litigation is also be used for harassment and extortion.

These bad practices have led to suits that are outright frauds. On March 7, 2014, a California appellate court upheld a trial judge's finding that what had been billed as a watershed liability verdict against Dole Food over pesticide use in Nicaragua was actually the product of a conspiracy by corrupt plaintiff's lawyers.

A New York federal judge ruled hat a multibillion-dollar pollution judgment against Chevron in 2011 was so tainted by bribery and coercion that it wasn't worth the paper it was written on.

A prominent class-action injury lawyer faces mounting woes because of allegations that he faked thousands of damage claims against BP related to the 2010 Gulf of Mexico oil spill.

**Why haven't these bad practices been challenged?** Litigating attorneys don't want tort reform! They put money together to lobby Congress with big campaign donations. Attorneys who have been elected to Congress also support these abusive practices.

**Only a Constitutional Convention will bring much-needed tort reform that will save Americans billions in insurance premiums, restore our rights in court, and also be fair to the legal profession.**

In England, their legal system is centuries older than ours and continues to function providing efficient justice. English courts are not jammed with lawsuits, and barristers are treated with the respect their profession deserves.

In England, frivolous litigation has a downside. The losing party pays the winner's legal fees! Before a barrister will file suit, he or she must make sure the facts prove his client has a justified claim. If the suit is lost, their client must have the money to cover all the winner's trial costs. Sometimes a client is required to post a bond to assure payment, should the trial be lost. If a client loses and cannot pay, his attorney is personally responsible.

This sensible legal procedure reduces frivolous suits and the courts can focus on prompt justice. We need to adopt the proven British system and elevate the ethics in the practice of law.

American lawyers will argue this prevents a poor person from receiving justice. That is not true. If a case is truly sound, the attorney can work on a contingency fee. This Amendment will restore dignity to the practice of law, help clear our court dockets, and speed up litigation. It will save doctors, hospitals, and consumers billions in insurance fees.

### **Section 1.** REDUCE LITIGATION

The losing party in all litigation shall pay all of the winner's reasonable legal expenses, and if unable to pay, then the losing litigant's attorney(s) shall be responsible for said payment.

The sixth Amendment of our Constitution starts, "In all criminal prosecutions, the accused shall enjoy the right to a **speedy and public trial**, …" The speedy part is not happening. We need justice to be rendered in both civil and criminal cases with reasonable promptness. Delay often causes unjustified financial and emotional harm to one or both parties as well as the public. Law schools teach, *"Justice delayed is justice denied."*

Because most lawyers charge fees based on the *hours* they work, there is little incentive to hasten the process. Filing repeated continuances that delay trials occur far too frequently. Attorneys procrastinate in preparing themselves in a timely manner. Judges are sometimes lax in the performance of their duties, delaying trials. We need to focus our courts on providing timely justice.

## **Section 2.** PROMPT JUSTICE

Judges are required to expedite all cases in an appropriate manner. Defendants, plaintiffs, and judges shall each have the right to only one continuance so that trials shall not be unduly delayed.

Another area of abuse is the award of punitive damages in excessive amounts. Punitive damages are compensation in excess of actual damages (a form of punishment awarded in cases of malicious or willful misconduct). Settlements for damages, both personal and punitive, go to the defendant, but punitive damages are actually an <u>insult to the public interest</u>. Punitive damages are somewhat like a traffic ticket where the funds go to the general public.

## **Section 3.** FAIRNESS

Punitive damages shall be paid to the federal, state, or city government as appropriate, not to the defendant.

In all trials, civil or criminal, during trial, introductions and especially during summations, whether representing a plaintiff or defendant, attorneys are permitted to say anything to influence a jury. It may have little relationship to the facts in the case. It may not even be true! This technique is destructive to the precepts of justice and too often helps the guilty go free. Attorneys who do not respect legal ethics and truth should be subject to punishment for a breach of law.

## **Section 4.** LEGAL ETHICS

During trials, if attorneys make statements not relevant to the specific case, deliberately distort evidence, or include information unrelated to the trial, such that the consequences tend to obfuscate the truth, or exaggerate, minimize, or distort facts sufficient to cause a mistrial, the judge may fine or suspend the attorney from the practice of law for up to one year.

The Constitution charges our courts to determine if a law, or part of a law is Constitutional. If a law does not conform to the Constitution it is declared unconstitutional, void, and unenforceable.

Today, when interpreting the Constitution, Judges in the District, Appellate, and Supreme Courts view the Constitution as a "living document." Because our Courts have become *politicized,* the Constitution is interpreted with political agendas that stretch beyond the original meaning of our Founding Fathers. Here are three examples.

1. A Constitutional challenge was made against the Affordable Healthcare Act because it forced citizens to pay medical premiums and provided for penalties for failure to pay. In a five to four decision the Supreme Court ruled that the law was Constitutional because the payments were a "tax." By definition taxes are a levy on income or property. Politically, the Court wanted the law to be upheld so it broadened the definition of "taxes."

2. Another trial before the Supreme Court argued that corporations could not give money for election campaigns as it gave corporations too much influence. The politicians, who collect the corporate money to get elected, appoint judges. The Court ruled generously in favor of corporate permitting unlimited contributions for elections.

3. Most Americans want two-term limits for elected officials. Because a few states passed laws imposing term limits, professional politicians challenged the law before the Supreme Court. Our courts are

politicized. The Court struck down the state laws as unconstitutional thereby perpetuating and protecting the professional politicians in Washington.

Another problem is the excessive time and cost to test the Constitutionality of a law or judgment. Much damage can be done before a ruling can grant relief. A speedier means to file an appeal and receive quicker judgment may lessen both time and cost. This can be achieved by sending all Constitutional issues directly to the appellate courts leaving the District Courts to handle civil and criminal trials as in the past. An additional way to both expedite and assure Constitutional Accountability is to permit Congress to request a prompt decision directly from the Supreme Court.

Perhaps the biggest challenge is to stop the Supreme Court from straying from the intent of the Constitution. By requiring a super majority of judges to certify Constitutionality we may constrain judges from straying beyond the Constitution's original intent. Favorable rulings of constitutionality would require a unanimous decision by appellate courts and a six-judge majority of the Supreme Court. This also reduces the ability of political pressure influencing the courts.

## **Section 5.** SPEEDING CONSTITUTIONAL RULINGS

All Constitutional challenges as to law or court rulings shall proceed directly to the appellate courts where favorable decisions must be unanimous else the law or judgment is unconstitutional , and a favorable majority of six judges of the Supreme Court is required to rule that a law or lower court decision is constitutional else the law is unconstitutional.

Twenty-five members of the Congress may submit a law or judgment directly to the Supreme Court for a prompt ruling as to its constitutionality.

Some court decisions trample the wording of the Founding Fathers and pass beyond interpretation into legislation. This invades the authority of Congress because it is equivalent to legislation. We need to restore strict interpretation of the Constitution and limit the courts' tendency to legislate.

## **Section 6.** PREVENTING COURT ORDERED LEGISLATION

Federal courts are prohibited from ordering any remedy not already available under federal law.

In the past Presidents have attempted to appoint judges with a specific political philosophy. This has also tended to politicize our federal courts. We can more objectively screen the qualifications of judicial appointments by permitting a majority of the state governors to confirm all appointments. This allows the states to retain some sovereignty and encourage court neutrality.

Federal Judges serve for life. At the time our Constitution was written, the average life expectancy was 46. Serving for life has a different consequence today. Our longer life expectancies permit some Judges to remain on the bench beyond their ability to properly adjudicate. Others wait till the government is in the control of their political party to retire. They are "gaming the system."

An upper age limit for service by Judges is appropriate. Consultation with a number of experienced attorneys recommended age eighty. This is consistent with today's average life expectancy of 70 at birth.

## Section 7. FEDERAL JUDGES

The President shall nominate federal judges, a majority of the Senate shall recommend them for approval, and a majority of the governors of the states shall confirm them, the governors having forty-five days after Senate approval to reject the nomination in writing to the President or the nominee shall be deemed approved.

Federal judges must retire at age eighty.

It is appropriate that all legal documents be consistently in one language.

## Section 8. OFFICIAL LANGUAGE

The official language of the United States is English

# Chapter Six

# GOVERNMENT RESPONSIBILITIES

*"Experience hath shown, that even under the best forms (of government) those entrusted with power have, in time, and by slow operations, perverted it into tyranny. I am not a friend to a very energetic government. It is always oppressive. The course of history shows that as a government grows, liberty decreases. Government big enough to supply everything you need is big enough to take everything you have."*

Thomas Jefferson

## Section 1. GOVERNMENT NECESSITIES

Effective upon the ratification of this amendment, Congress shall pass new laws only to provide for national security, law and order, protection of personal freedoms, the ownership of property, the safety of citizens, maintaining open trade and free markets, unhampered communications, and construction of infrastructure and transportation capabilities.

## Section 2. GOVERNMENT LIMITATIONS

Congress shall pass no law that permits government to compete with or subsidize private sector businesses, charities, or individuals. Congress shall pass no new laws or expand existing laws whereby government provides products or services available in the private sector, limits private business activity, free markets, or the freedoms of the people.

## Section 3. IMPLEMENTATION

At the time this amendment is ratified, all laws providing social programs, welfare, and other benefits conflicting with this amendment must, within six years, be revised so that all benefits transition to full privatized in an orderly manner within the next twenty years.

The quote above by Thomas Jefferson, an attendee at our original Constitution Convention, suggests there was serious discussion as to what our government should do and not do. If there was a debate about giving free stuff to citizens, the Founding Fathers decided against such benefits, and there is not a whisper about it in our Constitution.

Our Founding Fathers understood human nature and how future politicians might pander to the public with free stuff to get reelection. Politicians quite naturally enjoy the recognition, benefits, and power that accompany their office. Eventually they discover that it is legal to tax and borrow to provide free stuff so voters will reelect them. Once it starts, the political parties compete to see who can promise voters enough free stuff to win elections. That's where we are today, winning is more important than good government.

This amendment will not suddenly end benefits in a heartless manner. The objective is to slowly transition presently supplied government services and benefits to the private sector where they will be of *better quality at a lower cost to the public*. More bang for the buck.

Here are two important questions that explain why privatization is best. Who gives you quicker service, your grocery store or the agency that renews your driver's license? Who is most efficient, the private sector or government? If you agree that the private sector is more efficient (and it is) all citizens will do better buying benefits there instead of from a costly Government bureaucracy. Let's cut the tax load on the working people and let them spend their money as they wish. This practical concept is well established as sound economics.

In his book, *The Naked Constitution*, Adam Freeman wrote, "Hundreds of billions of dollars have been sucked out of the private economy and redirected to the federal government to be doled out for purposes that are politically expedient, but flatly unconstitutional."

An editorial entitled "To The Rescue Of A Republic At A Crossroads" published in the August 15, 2013 issue of *Investors Business Daily* opined:

"The President can no longer control the enormous and ever-expanding bureaucracy functioning as a government by fiat. The legislative branch, so corrupted, so drunk by the allure of power, so disdainful of its constituents, is unable to stop its bankrupting ways. The judiciary is perhaps the worst. The Supreme Court is openly rejecting the authority of the Constitution itself."

Our Founding Fathers thought a responsible government <u>should only do that which the Citizens **could not do** for themselves.</u> The Constitution does not provide for **entitlements,** yet seventy percent of government spending is entitlements.

Let's start with Section 1 of this amendment. What are the essential needs that ONLY government can fulfill? Congress calls them "discretionary," yet these are the *must have* functions of government. Without reform or other changes, entitlements will soon completely crowd out all of the essential discretionary spending within the next decade. Worst still, the focus on nondiscretionary spending (welfare) has distracted our government from doing the essentials. As you read these essentials, evaluate how well our government is performing them. These are the essentials that citizens need government to do because they cannot do it themselves?

### ESSENTIAL GOVERNMENT FUNCTIONS

NATIONAL SECURITY. The first obligation of every government is to provide for the peace and safety of its people, control of all borders, and protection from foreign forces. This means providing our military with the best and most advanced equipment, technology and training. History has proven that only strength keeps the peace.

LAW AND ORDER. Domestic tranquility and safety requires an honest, efficient and professional police force, good district attorneys to prosecute, honest courts dispensing prompt justice, and jails to incarcerate the violent and keep them from harming the public.

INFRASTRUCTURE. Essential for commerce and travel are good highways, railroads, bridges, navigable rivers, electric and gas power, and modern airports.

COMMUNICATIONS. The full free and rapid flow of all communications so citizens can dependably conduct business and enjoy the unhampered sharing of information.

FINANCIAL STABILITY. We need stable money, balanced budgets, a sound banking system, and prudent government policies that inspire confidence, and encourage entrepreneurs to expand trade, manufacturing, innovation, investment, and real job growth in private sector.

FREE MARKETS. Government must maintain competitive markets where prices are determined by supply and demand by mutual consent, never by force. Monopolies, oligopolies, and subsidies prevent the competitive flow of goods and services to consumers.

## **Section 1.** GOVERNMENT NECESSITIES

Effective upon the ratification of this amendment, Congress shall pass new laws only to provide for national security, law and order, protection of personal freedoms, the ownership of property, the safety of citizens, maintaining open trade and free markets, unhampered communications, and construction of infrastructure and transportation capabilities.

## IS THE UNITED STATES SIDETRACKED FROM ITS MISSION?

Americans have big hearts for helping people in need. Are we doing it the right way? Are our well-intended social programs truly helping people and reducing poverty? Is our government distracted from the essential services envisioned by our Founding Fathers?

On December 11, 1974, Friedrich A. Hayek in receiving his Nobel Prize in economics said this about government, "To act on the belief that we possess the knowledge and power which enable us to shape the processes of society entirely to our liking, knowledge which in fact we do not possess, is likely to make us do much harm."

Is our government too involved in social planning without understanding the downside unpredictable consequences?

Are foreign wars truly in our national interest? Should we expect our military to do nation building? Do our foreign conflicts have a clearly obtainable military objective for our country? Can we continue to sacrifice the blood of our soldiers and fritter away our national wealth? Isn't it the responsibility of citizens of each nation to fight for the kind of government they want for themselves?

Are our streets truly safe from crime? Why should we have the world's highest percentage of our population in jail while crime still runs rampant?

Are our roads and bridges ageing and in need of expansion and repair? Japan and China have high-speed trains running at over 300 miles-per-hour. Europe has high-speed 100 miles-per-hour highways for safe driving. We don't.

Expensive government subsidies interfere with free markets. We pay taxes to subsidize higher food prices at the supermarket. We even pay farmers money not to plant acreage. The Farm Bureau has more employees than we have farmers.

Why is our government failing to deliver on its primary responsibilities?

> OUR GOVERNMENT IS TOO INVOLVED IN ACTIVITIES
> FOR WHICH IT IS NOT QUALIFIED.
> WE CAN DO THESE THINGS BETTER OURSELVES
> AND WITH LESS COST!

*Our Constitution provides each of us the **opportunities to life, liberty and the pursuit of happiness.** It assumes **People are responsible to take care of themselves and their families.*** As a free people we want every opportunity to achieve success based on our God-given talents, education, honest work, and then the right to keep the fruits of our labor. Our Constitution does <u>not</u> promise <u>food, clothing, shelter, retirement, and free medicine</u>. People who think government can provide these things better than we can for ourselves are unrealistic and don't know history.

How did people suffering hardship survive <u>before government got involved with "welfare programs?"</u> Private charities funded by many citizens including the wealthy, helped people survive and become responsible and independent.

In the first two hundred years of our nation, when millions of immigrants came to our country, there were no welfare programs. With only a "sponsor," immigrants came from many countries speaking different languages. They quickly learned English, found jobs and became a working part of America. Church kitchens eased hunger when people had no job. Hospitals had free clinics providing care for the poor. The three-generational family was strong with grandparents and parents providing to their children loving care, good morals, and teaching the American work ethic from generation to generation. The three-generational family retired the elderly with dignity and love.

CHARITY *is the personal and voluntary* giving of money and/or time by *people* and *private organizations* <u>helping others survive, and become self-sufficient.</u> Today many private charities remain very active, funded with billions of dollars given by generous Americans. These charities provide professional assistance for a reasonable period of time to help people become independent. Americans have great compassion donating generously for those who are hungry, unable to care for themselves, need medical care, or are temporarily unemployed.

CHARITY is NOT the responsibility of government, paid for by forcibly taxing the working people to fund giant inefficient bureaucratic welfare programs. Government employees who run the system have a conflict of interest. If they help people on welfare to become independent, their job becomes obsolete. Inefficient government programs have reached cost levels that our economy can no longer sustain, and are growing rapidly. Food stamps and disability benefits are at all-time highs and the programs are filled with fraud, ineffective controls, and little accountability.

Well-intended welfare and poor educational programs have actually increased our impoverished illiterate population dependent on government from birth to grave and from generation to generation. The programs have sponsored aid for unwed mothers. It is estimated that over 70% of Black children are born out of wedlock, receiving too little love and discipline, and poor education. This accounts for their high level of crime and imprisonment. Despite the spending of trillions of dollars, the welfare programs are a failure. Poverty levels today are much the same as they were in 1960 when these programs were started. The <u>unintended consequences have been destructive morally and financially to our society</u>.

We have created a large number of *undeserving poor*. These are healthy people who game the benefit system and live in survivable poverty without working. It is impossible to know how many able-bodied millions are living off of the work of their fellow citizens. It is unfair, a moral disgrace, and financially unaffordable. It incentivizes poverty.

Social Security has taken hundreds of billions of dollars from Americans' paychecks to be deposited in a retirement trust fund. The average annual return has been about 2-1/2% as compared to over 11% in the stock market. Inflation has been greater than the return on Social Security.

Michael Cembalest, a research expert with J.P. Morgan, suggests that citizens turning 65 in 2013 will receive $327,500 in benefits in their lifetime. Yet future unborn children will pay in $421,000 more than they will receive. Social Security is neither social nor secure. It has replaced the Three Generational Family. If Social Security were privatized like our 401(k) programs, retirement would be far more generous and without a government bureaucracy.

The combination of unemployment, food stamps, disability, subsidized housing, and other benefits like free phones reduce the necessity to find a job and do productive work. Some people have received unemployment checks for two years and have lost their work ethic. The cost of government health is soaring.

Benefits to unmarried pregnant women, often teen-agers, provide incentives to have children out of wedlock. According to Senator Coburn, at the end of the Civil War, only 2% of Caucasian and 4% of Black children were born out of wedlock. In New Orleans currently over 20% of white children and over 50% of black children are born out of wedlock. Nationally, 2 of 5 births are to unmarried women. Too often children of single-parent families end up in street gangs as criminals dealing in illegal drugs and violence.

Food stamps replace church food kitchens and not only do they encourage obesity, but are too often sold at discount for cash to buy drugs.

Tax "refunds" go to low-income families who have actually paid no taxes, an invitation for fraud and avoiding self-betterment.

By what right should homeowners who work to pay their mortgage have to pay taxes for others to live in free or subsidized housing? Why should the government be in the housing business?

There are always truly needy people who are unable to care for themselves, and genuinely do need help. Before government, that help was and remains available in private charities, provided in a manner designed to help people to become independent.

Nothing is really free. Someone must produce the food people buy with food stamps. Qualified doctors and nurses are essential to the delivery of good medical care. The increasing cost of these programs will ultimately send our great nation into financial embarrassment. We are transitioning toward a failed economic system -- socialism.

**SOCIALISM** induces people to live in survivable poverty ignorant of opportunity or their personal potential for growth. Socialism sidetracks capable people from a good life to an unproductive dead-end existence without hope or ambition. Socialism leads to national bankruptcy like the Soviet Union, poverty as in Cuba, and starvation as in North Korea.

**FREE ENTERPRISE** is not free. It requires competitive work, efficient productivity, a wise investment of capital, and the right of ownership.

**FREE ENTERPRISE produces the most prosperity for the most people.**

This amendment is designed to prevent Congress from passing additional laws that move us toward more social benefits. The intended trend is toward Free Enterprise.

### **Section 2.** GOVERNMENT LIMITATIONS

Congress shall pass no law that permits government to compete with or subsidize private sector businesses, charities, or individuals. Congress shall pass no new laws or expand existing laws whereby government provides products or services available in the private sector, limits private business activity, free markets, or the freedoms of the people.

The final section of this amendment is intended to move government out of all social welfare programs and to peacefully transition to privatized benefits. Have no doubt that government programs can be <u>privatized</u> and with very favorable results.

Welfare and entitlement programs can be cut in a gentle and highly constructive manner. Here's proof! Newt Gingrich and President Bill Clinton did it very slowly in an orderly way in the 1990's. Gradually people came off of government dependency, found jobs, and actually paid taxes. Soon we had a huge surplus and prosperity. Smaller government benefits everyone. Here are some examples of how we can reduce the size of government with wonderful results.

The U.S. Post Office is losing billions annually and is hampered by political benefits to special interests. If it were to be incorporated and sold as a public company the cash billions our government would receive could be used to reduce our debt. Once privatized and free of political limitations, the privately run post office could earn a profit and pay taxes just like FEDEX.

Public housing can be converted to condominiums. Margaret Thatcher did it in Great Britain producing prosperity and growth. So can we.

Our Federal Government subsidizes railroads and streetcar systems. They too can be privatized with less waste, improved transportation, earn profits and pay taxes.

Social Security can be privatized over time and simultaneously make certain the benefits are 100% dependable. We need to gradually raise the retirement age to match the average life expectancy. Using time steps we would reschedule retirement from 65 to 79 with annual automatic adjustments to the average life expectancy. People are living longer, are able to work longer, and healthy enough to do it. Moreover, staying active tends to help maintain both mental and physical health. The present moneys from both workers and their employers would gradually transition into private investment accounts with retirement tax benefits.

| PRESENT AGE | NEW RETIREMENT AGE |
|---|---|
| 60 and up | No Change |
| 55-60 | 67 |
| 50-55 | 71 |
| 45-50 | 75 |
| 40-45 | 79 and recalculated to average life expectancy annually |
| 20-40 | average life expectancy with right to put half into 401K Roth |
| <20 | privatize half or all of social security donations into 401K |

Unemployment can also be privatized. Companies that discharge an employee would be required to pay six weeks at 75% of full average pay, then six weeks at half average pay, and a final six weeks at 25% of average pay. This doesn't require government to make any payment and it would step in only if the business were to declare bankruptcy. It puts into place a reasonable safety net, but also forces the employee to look for a new job.

Healthcare and disability insurance are in critical need of serious reform. Presently insurers are limited to states rather than the nation. Several financially sound national private insurers should compete for business directly to the consumer. This would eliminate the huge and growing government bureaucracy and save taxpayers billions with more customized coverage.

Education is the benefit where we need most urgently to get the federal government completely out! It is dangerous to have a central government controlling what our children are taught. The federal government has required that schoolbooks must have been written and printed within the last ten years. The old books are gone and history has been rewritten to appeal to socialists. In these books our country has done evil things and Free Enterprise is for greedy businessmen.

Education is a grass roots business between parents, teachers, students and administrators. Let's have the government give back all moneys designated for education directly to the states without strings. Let's reduce the money and the taxes that raise it in equal 20% increments over five years and have Uncle Sugar exit education completely.

There are many other kinds of benefits people use to manipulate and qualify for to live with higher incomes than those who work on the minimum wage. Perhaps a maximum combined benefit should be established at 70% of the minimum wage per person.

These suggested changes are intended to give readers examples of how we can make peaceful changes that get people back to work, end excessive out of wedlock births, restore financial solvency to our nation, and many other improvements.

It will only happen if we make it illegal for the government to do anything other than what we need it to do. We must stop professional politicians from pandering for votes with free benefits at the expense of working taxpayers. We must stop deficit spending and establish financial discipline so the essentials can be properly provided. These needed changes will be achieved only if we engrave them in our Constitution.

## **Section 3.** IMPLEMENTATION

At the time this amendment is ratified, all laws providing social programs, welfare, and other benefits conflicting with this amendment must, within six years, be revised so that all benefits transition to full privatized in an orderly manner within the next twenty years.

# Chapter Seven

# FINANCIAL STABILITY

*"A democracy cannot exist as a permanent form of government. It can only exist until the voters discover that they can vote themselves largesse from the public treasury. From that moment on, the majority always votes for the candidates promising the most benefits from the public treasury with the result that a democracy always collapses over loose fiscal policy, always followed by a dictatorship."*

"The Cycle of Democracy" Alexander Fraser Tyler
Scottish lawyer and writer, 1770

*"The democracy will cease to exist when you take away from those who are willing to work and give to those who would not."*

Thomas Jefferson

## Section 1. LIMITING TAXATION

All legislation that increases taxation or revenues must be passed by no less than a 60% majority vote of both the House of Representatives and the senate.

## **Section 2.** BUDGET ACCOUNTING AND REPORTING

All departments of government shall report revenues and expenses in strict accordance with the Government Accounting Standards Board regulations. The annual budget is hereby defined as one that includes all revenues and expenses for that year only, without exception. No spending may be excluded or deferred to the future, and revenues may include only monies received in the fiscal year in which they are collected.

Congress shall complete each annual budget no less than 90 days prior to the commencement of the next fiscal year, and Congress may not adjourn until fulfilling this requirement.

The budget shall be immediately delivered to the general accounting office. It shall determine as quickly as possible if the budget is in balance.

## **Section 3.** FINANCIAL RESPONSIBILITY

Any elected or appointed person holding office during two consecutive years when the budget has not been balanced shall be permanently ineligible to run for reelection to any federal office. During the second year in which the budget in not balanced, all pay, perquisites, and benefits normally received by all members of congress and their staffs shall cease until the budget is balanced and no refund or back pay shall be forthcoming.

The balanced budget requirement shall be waived in each year that a two-thirds vote of Congress declares that the United States is at War.

### Section 4. A LIMITED LINE ITEM PRESIDENTIAL VETO

If the General Accounting Standards office declares that the budget is not in balance, then the President is authorized to use a line item veto on any portion of any law for that fiscal year sufficient to balance the budget. The Congress shall have thirty days to override each veto with a sixty percent majority vote of either House of Congress, or the spending cut must be fully implemented.

### Section 5. DOWNSIZING TOP DOWN

The Cabinet of the United States shall consist of no more than sixteen secretaries; each secretary shall have no more than five assistant secretaries; each assistant secretary shall have no more than five undersecretaries; and supervisors shall supervise no less than ten employees. This amendment is to be fully implemented within three years of its ratification.

## **Section 6.** RESPONSIBILITIY OF BANKERS

Whenever the government is required to restore financial solvency to a bank or financial institution, the officers of that bank may be held directly and personally responsible for civil and criminal failure to serve the public interest properly.

Most Americans want a Balanced Budget, but should that be in our Constitution? Rigid financial rules embedded in our Constitution might prove self-destructive. If we were at war would it be better to balance the budget and lose the war? During recessions, temporary deficits might be the medicine of recovery. Concepts that are too rigid, break. Our financial system needs to be stable but flexible. Also games can be played with the numbers to produce a "balanced budget" that is not really balanced.

Something must be done because throughout history nations do go broke, and we are not immune to financial mismanagement. As the leader of the Free World, we must keep our financial house in order and prevent default or there could be a worldwide financial crisis. There are some moderate methods to solve this challenge in the Constitution, yet retain the necessary flexibility.

Let's be practical. If Congress really had to balance the budget would they cut spending or raise taxes? Their history is to raise taxes and spend us back into another deficit, and then call for more taxes. Tax/spend, tax/spend, it never ends. So first, let's consider putting more discipline on all means of revenue increases of any kind.

## **Section 1.** LIMITING TAXATION

All legislation that increases taxation or revenues must be passed by no less than a 60% majority vote of both the House of Representatives and the senate.

It has been several years since Congress has produced a budget even though they are required by law to do so. Continuing resolutions have become the budget substitute, permitting Congress to keep spending. It shows us the arrogance of our professional politicians that they ignore their own laws.

To have a real budget we have to establish accounting procedures to correctly calculate the budget, an annual time frame for the budget, and a credible agency to authenticate that the budget is balanced.

## **Section 2.** BUDGET ACCOUNTING AND REPORTING

All departments of government shall report revenues and expenses in strict accordance with the Government Accounting Standards Board regulations. The annual budget is hereby defined as one that includes all revenues and expenses for that year only, without exception. No spending may be excluded or deferred to the future, and revenues may include only monies received in the fiscal year in which they are collected.

Congress shall complete each annual budget no less than 90 days prior to the commencement of the next fiscal year, and Congress may not adjourn until fulfilling this requirement.

The budget shall be immediately delivered to the general accounting office that shall determine as quickly as possible if the budget is in balance.

To achieve a balanced budget, spending must be brought under control - and that requires Congressional discipline!

We need clear Constitutional goals and guidelines that will genuinely motivate elected officials to maintain financial discipline.

### **Section 3.** FINANCIAL RESPONSIBILITY
Any elected or appointed person holding office during two consecutive years when the budget has not been balanced shall be permanently ineligible to run for reelection to any federal office. During the second year in which the budget in not balanced, all pay, perquisites, and benefits normally received by all members of congress and their staffs shall cease until the budget is balanced and no refund or back pay shall be forthcoming.

The balanced budget requirement shall be waived in each year that a two-thirds vote of Congress declares that the United States is at War.

To further assist in balancing the budget let's give the President line item veto subject to Congressional oversight. This should improve the teamwork between the President and the Congress. It is a compromise worth considering. Congress will not want to be at the mercy of a Presidential line item veto that might cut their favorite legislation, so Congress needs powers to redress Presidential line item vetoes.

## **Section 4.** A LIMITED LINE ITEM PRESIDENTIAL VETO

If the General Accounting Standards office declares that the budget is not in balance, then the President is authorized to use a line item veto on any portion of any law for that fiscal year sufficient to balance the budget. The Congress shall have thirty days to override each veto with a sixty percent majority vote of either House of Congress, or the spending cut must be fully implemented.

Most Americans know our government is too big, but are uninformed as to how much it has grown. We won World War II in four years with a Cabinet of 10 secretaries plus the Vice President. Today our Cabinet has

33 secretaries plus the Vice President. Our government has tripled its size!

Washington has layers of personnel structure that hamper communications and efficiency. In business the chain-of-command is usually limited to five layers. Our government has as many as ten.

When a business is in financial trouble and has to cut costs, it does it from the top down. That means the cuts are made from the most highly paid executives down to the lowest-paid workers. If the business is to survive, no one is spared review. Top down reductions must be applied to reduce the size of our government.

In the free market, the salary paid for any job depends on the value of that job, but not so in government. Most government employees are now paid 30% to 50% more than their private sector counterpart, yet they may be less productive.

This Amendment seeks to correct government spending in a manner similar to the policies used in the private sector.

## **Section 5.** DOWNSIZING TOP DOWN

The Cabinet of the United States shall consist of no more than sixteen secretaries; each secretary shall have no more than five assistant secretaries; each assistant secretary shall have no more than five undersecretaries; and supervisors shall supervise no less than ten employees. This amendment is to be fully implemented within three years of its ratification.

The banking industry is given very special treatment under law. Debts owed to banks are considered "senior debt" taking preference for payment ahead of all other kinds of debt. In addition, banks have a privileged position in our economy in that they can lend money created out of thin air as deposits. Banking is one of the most profitable industries in our country.

When bank executives extend excessive credit or take inappropriate risks such that their bank must be bailed out by the federal government whereby the public suffers the losses, the corporate shield protects them. The crash of 2008-9 saw major financial institutions collapse costing the public trillions in losses, yet no one was prosecuted.

Banking is a critical part of our economy and deserves its special support such that debt owed is repaid, but bankers must also be held responsible for lending that money in a prudent manner, and no longer be shielded from failure to protect the public interest.

### **Section 6.** RESPONSIBILITIY OF BANKERS

Whenever the government is required to restore financial solvency to a bank or financial institution, the officers of that bank may be held directly and personally responsible for civil and criminal failure to serve the public interest properly.

# Chapter Eight

# LAW AND ORDER

*"Let the punishment fit the crime."*

Gilbert and Sullivan

## Section 1. CRIME DEFINED

Crime is hereby defined as a threat or act of violence against the nation, persons, or property without consent.

## Section 2. CONSENSUAL CONTRACTS ARE LEGAL

Congress shall make no laws that criminalize consensual transactions.

## Section 3. PROTECTING VICTIMS

Persons committing any crime, regardless of age or mental capability, shall be presumed to know the difference between right and wrong and shall be held responsible for breaking the law. Criminal records may not be expunged unless a conviction is reversed.

## **Section 4.** ELIMINATE LEGAL EXCUSES

All trials and appeals related to criminal guilt or innocence shall focus on the facts, truth, and proof; errors of procedure or legal performance shall not serve to annul a verdict and conviction, except where law enforcement officials can be proven not to have performed as required by law.

## **Section 5.** PROMPT PUNISHMENT

All criminals shall commence serving their sentence at the time of conviction. Any judge unable to determine the sentence at the time of conviction shall do so within thirty days after conviction and the time in prison shall be counted against the sentence.

## **Section 6.** PUNISHMENT FOR MURDER AND SPEEDY APPEALS

Persons convicted of first-degree murder will be sentenced as adults regardless of intention, age or mental health. Sentence shall be rendered no later than thirty days after conviction, and carried out within three months, subject to appeal. All criminal appeals must be filed within three months after conviction and judgment on the appeal rendered within three months.

Have you ever had something stolen or experienced an act of violence? If so, do you remember the deep feelings of unfairness and being violated? Do you remember what it was like to be a victim? Were you angry?

We no longer live in the days of the "Wild West" when everyone carried a "six-shooter." As a civilized people, we have generally given up carrying weapons because we have the police, prosecutors, and judges to protect us. Are they doing their jobs? Do we feel safe when we go for a walk on the street at night? Are our police and courts controlling crime and providing law and order? Are the prosecutors and judges keeping criminals off the streets? Is Justice being meted out promptly? Are criminals apprehended, tried, convicted and punished properly, *or is the system broken?*

Are criminals getting more "justice" than their victims?

Criminals hurt people. You and I wouldn't hurt anyone, but criminals do because they think differently. Criminals are brutal people and feel little remorse or guilt for their actions. Somehow we seem to have forgotten that truth. Most Americans consider our country so wealthy and civilized that must deal with criminals in a humane manner. Is that consistent with the criminal mind? To control crime we need laws that criminals can understand, real enforcement, conviction and punishment. When there is deterrence, criminals respect the law.

## **REALLY REDUCING CRIME**

Our biggest cause of crime is illegal drugs. Ask any sheriff and he will confirm that over half of the crimes of violence are drug-related. Drug convictions also account for the largest number of criminals in our jails. Habitual drugs are illegal yet they are available throughout the United States.

Americans do not understand what crimes can be enforced, and what crimes are unenforceable. The sale of illegal drugs is an excellent example. Is the sale of an illegal drug an act of violence? Is there a victim?

What is and is not a crime? Today our society does not deal with crime in a manner consistent with human nature because we don't understand the correct answers to those important questions.

There are two kinds of crimes.

**REAL CRIME is:** *"A threat or act of violence against our nation, person(s) or property without consent."* Please think about that definition. It fits with human nature. This definition of crime is enforceable because there is a **victim and an act of violence**. Essential to prosecuting a criminal is a **victim** willing to testify in court against him for an **act of violence**. This is the kind of crime that we need to control.

**LEGISLATED CRIME is:** *"A transaction or activity done between two or more persons by mutual consent but is against the law."*

Laws can be passed to criminalize anything, but the law must be consistent with human behavior or it is **unenforceable**. A law can be passed that we may eat only one meal a day, but few will obey. Almost every state in the nation has a law against fornication outside of marriage. The police don't even try to enforce such a foolish law because it is so blatantly inconsistent with human nature and unenforceable. This even applies to our Constitution!

The 18th Article of Amendment to our Constitution called "prohibition" was passed on January 29, 1919. It read in part: *"After one year from the ratification of this article, the manufacture, sale, or transportation of intoxicating liquors within, the importation thereof into, or the exportation thereof from the United States and all territory subject to the jurisdiction thereof for beverage purposes is hereby prohibited."*

It quickly proved to be so unenforceable and caused so many problems, it was repealed <u>14 years later!</u> On December 5, 1933 our 21st Amendment read: *"The Eighteenth Article of Amendment to the Constitution of the United States is hereby repealed."*

A Constitutional law, the Highest Law of the Land, <u>simply didn't work!</u> Alcoholism can eventually kill a person, but making alcoholic beverages illegal did not stop their use. Prohibition just made liquor less available, more expensive to buy and often of dangerous quality.

## UNINTENDED CONSEQUENCES

Supporters of Prohibition thought that they were doing the "right thing' for society. Yet the unintended consequences actually make conditions worse.

Unenforceable laws produce havoc. As soon as alcoholic beverages became illegal, free market competition no longer regulated price or quality, and government no longer collected taxes. The flow of alcohol never stopped, it went underground to secret bars called "Speakeasies." They made huge profits selling drinks of poorer quality at higher prices and some drinks were actually deadly.

The purchase/sale of an alcoholic beverage is a transaction made by the mutual consent of the buyer and seller. There is no victim so the law is unenforceable. Any time something that people want is made illegal, the high profitability will attract a black market supply. Prohibition profits were so lush that for the first time racketeers were able to form a national criminal organization providing illegal liquor. Distributors started killing each other over territorial rights. Law enforcement failed because drinkers refused to testify (they weren't victims), and payoffs to politicians, judges and police for protection to bootleggers corrupted our law enforcement system.

That criminal structure remains today, providing illegal drugs that are just as unenforceable as was alcohol. Today, marijuana, heroin, "angel dust," and other natural and synthetic illegal drugs are sold in every city in our country. The quality is unreliable, the prices are high, profits are huge, and no taxes are paid. It fosters the majority of the crimes of violence as distributors again kill each other over territorial rights. Innocents citizens are also hurt and killed when habitual drug users mug, rob, break into homes, steal cars, and commit violent crimes to raise money to feed their habits.

It is an international business. Illegal drugs finance the Mexican cartels, the commerce of Colombia, the poppy farmers in Afghanistan, and even help finance the Taliban.

The police know they can't control it any better than they could Prohibition. In addition, money compromises law enforcement personnel, politicians and judges. Yet some do try to enforce the unenforceable.

Genuine efforts to enforce drug laws have resulted in a terrible loss of life among law enforcement personnel. In 2009, 122 federal, state and local law enforcement personnel were killed seeking to enforce drug laws. In 2010 there were 153 deaths in the line of duty. In 2012 the number increased again to 173, a needless loss of life of officers that would probably be alive if all drugs were legalized, regulated, and taxed. Government spending to stop illegal drug traffic runs over $20 billion annually. This money could be spent elsewhere, or used to reduce the deficit.

More and more Americans are in favor of the practical policy of legalizing drugs. Marijuana is just the beginning. Anyone who tries to legalize drugs makes powerful underworld enemies. That's because the illegal drug business is very profitable, with no taxes paid. It is so profitable that smugglers build submarines and buy airplanes to secretly transport drugs into our country.

Drug buyers and sellers are the largest criminal sector in our jails for doing a *consensual* business where there was no victim, no coercion, and *no act of violence*.

The dollar cost of incarcerating drug offenders is in the billions. Many of our prisons are run as private businesses. The sheriffs are paid an incentive for each prisoner because our prisons need to maintain a high level of occupancy to be profitable. Our incarcerated population remains abnormally high as a percentage of our population.

**Legalizing all drugs would lower their prices, improve quality, provide a new tax base for government, and see at least a 50% decline in crimes.** Many countries have areas where any drug can be bought legally. Other countries provide them at drug stores like any other medicine, and that is what we should do. Cheaper, better quality drugs would substantially reduce the need for users to commit violent crimes to finance their habit. The drug distributors would go out of business and drug-related killings would stop. Without distributors, marketing legal drugs to entice youngsters to do "social" or "macho" drugs is gone.

Many drug users and distributors presently in jail, having never committed a single violent crime, could be pardoned and released. They could find decent jobs and become part of society again. We would save billions in jail expenses and there would be plenty of room for real criminals who commit acts of violence.

Idealistic people will object to making these drugs legal because they are dangerous, and they are. Making quality drugs legally available at competitive prices will cause some users to overdose and die. But we are a free people, and that is part of our freedom. We must be responsible for the consequences of our decisions and actions. Smokers and alcoholics know they risk cancer and death, but that choice is part of their freedom. We are free as long as we do not invade the freedoms of others.

Why are politicians silent on drug legalization? Because they would lose the votes of many who don't understand that consensual agreements are not crimes. In addition, underworld interests protect their markets by giving election donations through third intermediaries. That money buys political silence. Did you hear any politician discuss legalizing drugs in the 2012 national elections? Elected officials and sheriffs know the public will not obey unrealistic laws, but few are willing to support legalization from fear of retribution by the drug syndicates.

The trend of the future is clear. Colorado's legalized pot sales are seen at about $1 billion this fiscal year with $40 million in tax revenues. People want it and government authorities like the tax income. The majority of people under age 40 want these drugs legalized. As time passes that opinion will grow stronger and eventually dominate. I believe that within a decade the public demand on politicians will be so strong that all drugs will gradually be legalized. It already has momentum that will be impossible to stop.

Perhaps the best way to legalize all drugs is a compromise with the businessmen who are already bringing drugs into our country. It would provide them with <u>legal</u> territorial franchises to distribute quality drugs through drug stores at competitive prices. They could negotiate more aggressively with foreign suppliers, so import costs would drop sharply. Manufacturing would be streamlined, quality improved, bribes saved, distribution inexpensive, and they would be heroes by ending most drug-related crimes.

This concept should be extended to all consensual crimes with the same excellent results for all concerned. Prostitution is another example. Why not legalize the oldest profession? We tax most everything else that moves, why not sex?

Morals are best enforced by our religions. What law is strongest in guiding our moral behavior—God's law or Government's law?

When enforcement of morals is assigned to government, it weakens the authority of our churches, synagogues, temples, and mosques. Historically, governments controlled by religions have been the most oppressive to all freedoms.

<u>**We need to focus on the crimes of violence that are enforceable!**</u> This is consistent with human nature and will change the entire crime and prison profile of our nation. The best way to reduce violent crime of all

kinds is to specify more clearly in our Constitution what is and is not a crime, and what cannot be made into a crime.

## Section 1. CRIME DEFINED

Crime is hereby defined as a threat or act of violence against the nation, persons, or property without consent.

## Section 2. CONSENSUAL CONTRACTS ARE LEGAL

Congress shall make no laws that criminalize consensual transactions.

Let's address real crime. The cruelest crime is murder. Murder deprives a person of many years of life. How we punish murderers sets the standard of deterrence against all lesser crimes. Do we punish murder in a way that generates deterrence? Do murderers fear punishment?

In Chicago, three teens played a game called "pick 'em out and knock 'em out." The three attacked Mr. Mora, beat him to death and stole his money. They had no moral hesitation about committing the murder, and the threat of punishment was so weak that they actually posted a video of their murder on the Internet.

Criminals use force to take what they want. They don't expect to get caught, and there is little fear of real punishment even if caught and prosecuted. They express little guilt or remorse for their victims; only regret that they were caught. Our society's concern about convicting an innocent person has made it very difficult to convict dangerous criminals. The guilty escape punishment, and without fear of punishment, deterrence is an illusion.

Below are numbers as reported on the Internet. Violent crimes include: Damage to Property, Rape, Robbery, Assault, Burglary, Larceny, and Car Theft. Murder numbers are separate.

| YEAR | TOTAL ALL CRIMES | MURDER |
|------|------------------|--------|
| 1960 | 3,384,200 | 9,110 |
| 1970 | 8,098,000 | 16,000 |
| 1980 | 13,408,300 | 23,040 |
| 1990 | 14,475,600 | 23,440 |
| 2000 | 11,608,072 | 15,586 |
| 2010 | 10,329,135 | 14,748 |

During 2000 there were 15,586 murders and 85 executions in the United States. A decade later in 2010 there were 14,748 murders and 46 executions. Only one murderer is executed for every 320 murders! That's less than a one-third of one percent chance that a murderer will be executed for their crime. With only one chance in 320 of being executed there is virtually zero deterrence. Why should criminals worry about punishment for lesser crimes?

Per capita dollar losses for crime in the U.S. are among the highest in the world. It is impossible to put a dollar value on the terrible emotional stress and unhappiness of victims. The main reason is because in an effort to protect the innocent, new legal hurdles to convict clearly guilty criminals have hampered the ability to obtain convictions. That has further reduced criminals' fear of consequences.

**We need to <u>restore</u> sufficient legal powers to our law enforcement officials, our system of prosecution, and court procedures so that perpetrators face real justice and punishment for their crimes.**

The word <u>restore</u> is accurate because in the early years of our country, punishment for criminals was more certain, swift and severe. It deterred crime, and there was very little! People could leave their home unlocked overnight, and safely walk the streets at night. Gradually changes in the procedures of arrest, prosecution, trial, and punishment have crippled law enforcement.

Somehow we forgot about the victims. Despite the suffering of the victim, Government provides little damage recovery but spends plenty to protect and incarcerate criminals. Today our justice system places fair treatment of the criminal ahead of the victim. Defense attorneys have greatly enhanced the legal protections criminals enjoy during prosecution. Convictions are hard to get, and executions for first degree murder nearly impossible. Public executions are gone because they are considered "cruel and unusual" punishment. The cruel treatment the murderers meted out to their victims is overlooked.

**Criminal trials have become a game of obfuscation rather than the search for truth, justice, and**

**punishment.** The focus today is on the intent and capability of the criminal, rather than what the criminal did to the victims and the proof of his/her guilt.

The Miranda decision is an excellent example. Why should the law have to warn a criminal who did something wrong? If a criminal kills, isn't it reasonable to assume that he or she is aware that it is murder? Why should written confessions that the law knows are accurate not be admissible if a criminal has not been read their rights? Victims deserve that the system of law enforcement is prompt in collecting the facts, and appropriate justice be meted out – no legal loopholes.

Yet, criminals are so adept at using legal procedures and precedents to claim an unfair trial that they have become amateur lawyers. They prepare their own appeals and pleadings, asserting that they are mentally ill, incompetent, claim ineffectual legal representation, or other legal ploys to seek a new trial or acquittal. Any breach of procedure can cause a mistrial. Here is an excellent example.

On Saturday, April 11, 2012 the headline in the New Orleans *Times-Picayune* newspaper read, "Trial No. 5 is set in '07 murder." The article reads in part, "Anthony Martin just wants his day in court. Not that he hasn't seen plenty of them."

"His first trial in August of 2007, for the fatal shooting of El Salvadorian laborer Julio Benitez Cruz ended in a mistrial, after one police officer was vacationing at Disneyland and another blurted out too much about

Martin's criminal past." All of his mistrials were because of legal or court gaffes.

Endless filings, delays and appeals cost the public millions of dollars. Time is on the side of the criminal. There is hope of getting a lenient judge that witnesses will fail to appear, die, or yield to threats and intimidation from criminal friends for testifying against the accused.

Crimes committed by minors harm their victims just as much as those committed by adults. Minors are treated with such leniency that it teaches a bad lesson. Upon reaching adulthood their criminal records are expunged. These experiences tell them that they can beat any rap.

To catch, indict, try, convict, sentence, and incarcerate a criminal today is so difficult that it truly protects the criminal more than the victim. Constitutional action is needed.

## Section 3. PROTECTING VICTIMS

Persons committing any crime, regardless of age or mental capability, shall be presumed to know the difference between right and wrong and shall be held responsible for breaking the law. Criminal records may not be expunged unless a conviction is reversed.

What is important is TRUTH. A crime is a crime, and if the accused can be proven to have done that criminal act, there should be *no excuses, no loopholes, no procedures that prevent* a swift trial and serious punishment. The *intentions* of the criminal should be secondary to the violence committed. Facts and proof must be restored to determining the basis of guilt or innocence, not legal procedures or ploys. Who did what to whom? Judges and juries should render their decisions based on the facts.

The scales of justice are weighted against the district attorney and the police. When conviction is difficult, the prosecution is forced to plea bargain so the criminal gets off easy. That defeats justice.

Certain that they have the guilty person but lacking sufficient evidence, law enforcement officials may hide or fabricate information to obtain conviction. That too is wrong. The prosecution must be just as focused on the truth as the defense, judge and jury.

## **Section 4.** ELIMINATE LEGAL EXCUSES

All trials and appeals related to criminal guilt or innocence shall focus on the facts, truth, and proof; errors of procedure or legal performance shall not serve to annul a verdict and conviction, except where law enforcement officials can be proven not to have performed as required by law.

Psychologists have repeatedly proven that we human beings respond to <u>reward</u> and <u>punishment</u>. The rewards for honesty and hard work are success, money, and a good reputation. Similarly, when bad behavior is quickly followed with real and memorable unpleasant punishment, it deters more bad behavior. Criminals must be held responsible for their actions.

In Asia the underage criminal is publicly "caned" and sent home. That means they are beaten with a stick, often a bamboo stick, on the legs and butt. It is a very painful, memorable, public punishment that they will not want repeated. The lesson is inexpensive for the state, over quickly, and has a lasting deterrent impact on the potential criminal. He does not spend months in jail with hardened criminals learning the wrong trade.

Today we have the Spock generation where the response to misbehavior is, "time out." Physical discipline is considered parental abuse, and parents can actually go to jail for disciplining their own children. We have probably gone from excessive punishment to excessive permissiveness. Too many children grow up not knowing or believing that there is punishment for criminal behavior.

We are a tough species, so punishment must be swift, certain, and severe if it is to be feared and produce deterrence. Criminals must know that if they hurt others they will receive an equal or greater hurt to themselves. Punishment in our justice system needs an overhaul.

Convicted criminals have many ways to delay serving their sentence. Shouldn't criminals go to jail as soon as they are convicted? Let the appeals start afterwards, but in fairness, punishment should be immediate to take the criminal off of the streets. Prompt punishment acts as a deterrent to other potential offenders.

## **Section 5.** PROMPT PUNISHMENT

All criminals shall commence serving their sentence at the time of conviction. Any judge unable to determine the sentence at the time of conviction shall do so within thirty days after conviction and the time in prison shall be counted against the sentence.

The appeal procedure is another area of abuse that is costly to the public. Repeated appeals, many without merit, can go on for years, and there are no limits to how many appeals a criminal can file. Often the criminals, including murderers, write their own appeals. Punishment for first-degree murder should not be delayed, as it is the worst of all crimes. It is very difficult for today's juries to convict a murderer in the first degree with no doubt of guilt. Yet first-degree murder sentences are followed by appeals averaging over 10 years, and are repetitive, costly, and abusive to the public interest.

## **Section 6.** PUNISHMENT FOR MURDER AND SPEEDY APPEALS

Persons convicted of first-degree murder will be sentenced as adults regardless of intention, age or mental health. Sentence shall be rendered no later than thirty days after conviction, and carried out within three months, subject to appeal. All criminal appeals must be filed within three months after conviction and judgment on the appeal rendered within three months.

# Chapter Nine

# THE COUNTERMAND AMENDMENT

## PROTECTING STATE SOVEREIGNITY

**Section 1.** State Legislatures, and/or Countermand Committees appointed by the Legislatures to act with full authority on their behalf when the Legislature is not in session, have the right to assert state sovereignty by passing and enforcing Countermand Resolutions when, a sufficient majority of State Legislatures determine that actions, regulations, laws, or the conduct of the Government or federal personnel exceed the authority granted by the states in the Constitution.

A majority vote shall be sufficient to immediately rescind any executive order, Presidential appointment, or government agency's regulatory ruling.

A two-thirds vote shall be sufficient to declare as Unconstitutional and null and void any Congressional Statute or Judicial decision.

A three-quarters vote shall be sufficient to immediately remove any elected official from office. Should the President be removed, his successor shall be immediately sworn into the office of President and Commander in Chief.

**Section 2.** From the time the initial State Legislature or its Countermand Committee issues a Countermand Resolution the other states shall have 24 months to reach the appropriate majority to approve the Resolution as described above, else the Resolution shall terminate.

**Section 3.** Each State Legislature must promptly complete their Countermand Resolution affidavit and deliver a certified copy to the Chief Justice of the United States Supreme Court, the Leader of the United States Senate, the Speaker of the House of Representatives, the President of the United States, and when applicable the Government Agency or Body and they shall be immediately responsible to enforce the Countermand.

**Section 4.** Any elected or appointed government official, or government employee, or any individual or organization, who intentionally obstructs or prevents the implementation of any provision in this Article shall have committed a criminal offense and shall be subject to impeachment (when applicable) and criminal prosecution, and upon conviction, shall serve no less than five years in prison.

**Section 5.** Should Federal prosecution of offenders of this Amendment not be initiated and concluded within one year from the date a Countermand Resolution having been approved, all States shall have the authority to prosecute violators of this Article under State laws. Multiple prosecutions, by multiple States, for the same alleged crime are prohibited.

**Section 6.** This Article shall immediately become part of the United States Constitution upon ratification by three quarters of the State Legislatures among the several States.

**Section 7.** The provisions of this Article are enforceable within all States of the United States including the District of Columbia, the Commonwealth of Puerto Rico, the Commonwealth of the Northern Mariana Islands and the territories and possessions of the United States.

In our country sovereignty derives from the People. The People granted limited powers to the States, and when the States ratified our Constitution they granted limited powers to the Federal Government. Over the past several decades our federal government has gathered to itself more and more power not intended by the Constitution.

The Federal Government taxes the states and then grants their own money back to them only if they follow regulations issued by the Federal Government. Some laws and regulations of the Federal Government are considered undesirable, counter productive, and even offensive by the states because they unfavorably impact the culture, freedoms and opportunities of the people. The states need a reasonable Constitutional means to redress the balance of power between the States and the Federal Government. The Countermand Amendment achieves this balance by permitting various levels of State Legislative majorities (including their Counterman Committees) to take the Constitutional actions necessary to reassert state sovereignty. The need is urgent and popular.

An Amendment similar to this has been very sponsored by Citizen Initiatives ably led by Charles Kacprowicz. Charles has traveled to almost every state to make the case that an Amendment is needed to balance political power between the Federal and State Governments.

The amendment here differs from that of the Citizen Initiative in that it increases the Countermand powers of the States as the size of the majority vote increases to address all levels of sovereign abuse. It permits the State Legislatures to appoint a Countermand Committee authorized to act promptly on behalf of the Legislature when not in recess. Finally, it provides two years for the states to redress federal abuses and sufficient power for the States to enforce Countermands on the Federal Government and to prosecute and sentence offenders of the Amendment.

Many patriotic Americans want to call a single issue Constitutional Convention for a Countermand Amendment or a Balanced Budget Amendment. It is clear that broader improvements are needed so that a single issue Convention is too limiting. It would be unable to address term limits, election reform, tort reform, and more. There is also real concern that a single issue Convention may "bolt" and run out of control.

The Resolution proposed in this book calls for an open Constitutional Convention with clear guidelines. It limits the Convention from becoming a "run away" Convention by prohibiting Amendments that affect the Bill of Rights, civil rights, or the creation of special privileges. More importantly, it invites the Convention to address many important issues that would enhance citizen freedoms and economic prosperity. Because ratification requires the approval of 38 states it is highly unlikely that an inappropriate Amendment will ever be ratified.

# Chapter Ten

# KEEPING THE CONSTITUTION CURRENT

When our country was founded there were only thirteen colonies and our small government had patriots as elected officials. The original path for amending the Constitution, through Congress, was used frequently. Now with fifty states, an oversized government, partisan party politics, the seniority system, and professional career politicians getting rich, Congress no longer makes the Constitutional changes necessary to keep our government current with the rapid technological and social changes.

Presently it requires two-thirds majority votes for Congress to propose a Constitutional Amendment. <u>We need to reduce the vote requirement of Article V to a lesser majority of 60%.</u> This would return to Congress the primary responsibility of keeping our Constitution current. Recommended Amendments would still have the necessary three-quarter state vote hurdle to be ratified.

Similarly, it takes two-thirds of the state legislatures to call a Constitutional Convention. <u>We need to reduce the number of state legislatures needed to call a Constitutional convention to 60% of the states.</u>

Mankind is doubling his knowledge about every three years. We need to keep our Constitution current with the rapidly changing times. The three-quarters hurdle will protect us from foolish and impractical Amendments.

## <u>AMEND ARTICLE V</u>

Article V shall be amended to read, "A <u>sixty percent</u> vote of both houses of Congress shall be sufficient to propose amendments to this Constitution…"

Sixty percent of the state legislatures shall be sufficient to call a Constitutional Convention…

A Constitutional Convention might also consider a third means to propose Amendments. For example, why not permit Amendments to be proposed for ratification by petitions with no less than five percent of the registered voters in one more than half of the states? It would then be subject to the usual three-quarters of the state legislatures for ratification.

# Chapter Eleven

# GOD BLESS AMERICA

## Section 1a. or 1b. FREEDOM OF RELIGIOUS EXPRESSION

Congress shall make no laws, nor may courts issue any religious rulings denying the peaceful and free expression of faith on public or private property.

**or**

Congress shall make no laws, nor may courts issue judgments denying the private or public expressions of worship.

In recent years civil rights groups have filed suits arguing that religious symbols and activities such as prayer in or on public property are unconstitutional. They suggest that a cross, the Ten Commandments, statues and religious activity on public property are inappropriate. They argue that it might offend the part of our population that is agnostic or atheist. As a consequence, court rulings have systematically reduced religion's traditional place in American culture. Congress refuses to address the issue, so again, action by a Constitutional Convention could clarify what the people want.

These suits and the judgments are well intended, but they ignore the fact that our system of government is based on the rule of the majority. We elect by majority. Congress passes laws by majority. Boards of Directors decide by majority. The concept is simple, the greater good for the greater number.

Our laws also argue that protecting the rights and freedoms of each citizen are more important than the majority. Without that legal precedent minorities or a individuals might be deprived of their personal freedoms.

Should courts rule to protect a minority or single individual to the detriment of the interests of the majority? Where is the balance between the group and the individual?

Perhaps the real issue is, does religion help our people live together in greater harmony, strengthen the family, and increase socially appropriate behavior? Doesn't religion teach us to treat each other as we want to be treated? Do we want to keep reducing that which helps us live together with less violence and greater harmony? The words "In God We Trust" appears on our money.

Our country's success is grounded on a Christian Judaic heritage. That system of beliefs has played a big part in building a great nation where people worship as they choose, respect each other's beliefs, and accept different ways of worship without interference. Our Founding Fathers wrote a Constitution that supports separation of church and state, not suppression of religion.

When it comes to religion, true freedom of worship means that an individual or a majority may not interfere with each other's freedom to worship! The government should simply stay out of it. Here are two possible Amendments that might address this question, and surely a Constitutional Convention will shine some light on the wording.

## **Section 2.** FREEDOM OF RELIGIOUS EXPRESSION

Congress shall make no laws, nor may courts issue any religious rulings denying the peaceful and free expression of faith on public or private property.

Congress shall make no laws, nor may courts issue judgments denying the private or public expressions of worship.

As long as we have "In God We Trust" on our money, let's keep him in our hearts and country, and hope that God will continue to bless America!

## Chapter Twelve

# WHAT KIND OF ECONOMIC SYSTEM DO WE WANT?

*"You cannot strengthen the weak by weakening the strong. You cannot further the brotherhood of man by encouraging class hatred. You cannot help the poor by destroying the rich. You cannot keep out of trouble by spending more than you earn. You cannot build character and courage by taking away man's initiative and independence. You cannot help men permanently by doing for them what they could and should do for themselves."*

Abraham Lincoln

*"The inherent vice of Capitalism is the unequal sharing of blessings, and the inherent blessing of Socialism is the equal sharing of misery."*

Winston Churchill

*"The problem with Socialism is that you eventually run out of other people's money."*

Margaret Thatcher

During the last century Mankind experimented with two economic models, Socialism and the Free Enterprise System. A comparison of the results proves that although Free Enterprise is not perfect, it clearly provides the most freedom, opportunity and prosperity for the most people. Socialism's repetitive track record is one of failure. The Soviet Union, the ultimate test of Socialism, failed miserably. The USSR collapsed and disappeared leaving a trail of hunger, cruelty, death, and financial default as its legacy. Today, Cuba suffers poverty and North Korea both poverty and starvation. At the end of this chapter you will see visual proof that Free Enterprise is the economic system of choice.

As the amount of free stuff increases it transitions a nation's economic system from Free Enterprise to Socialism. Why is Socialism a financially failed economic model? Worse still, why is it destructive to the social, moral, and work ethic of a people? When a nation embraces socialism the long-term consequences inevitably lead to financial default on all obligations or the total destruction of the money, or both. Many Americans do not understand the economic challenge that we face if we do not move away from Socialism and back to Free Enterprise.

While Socialism appeals to our ideals of equality for all, it doesn't work. The reasons are that it doesn't fit with human nature. People are not equal. Just like our fingerprints are unique, each of us is special with talents, skills, ideas and beliefs. To level equality on a people requires force. We can be forced into equality only with a dictatorship. Before its collapse the Soviet

Union was a giant inefficient uncompetitive prison of forced labor. Its workers risked death to climb the Berlin wall to seek freedom.

The biggest weakness of Socialism it that it denies people the right of ownership – the right to keep the fruits of our labor and spend it as we wish. Without the right of ownership, there is little incentive to work, create, and grow. The first tenant of Free Enterprise is the uninterrupted legal right of ownership. If we earn our money by producing something of value, the money belongs to us, as well as what we buy with it. Free Enterprise is everybody working according to their ability, being paid based on the value of what they produce, and the freedom to spend our money, invest, or give it away to charity if they wish.

Socialists like Karl Marx believe "From each according to his ability, to each according to his needs." They believe that government should decide what to take from those who work and have ability, and give it to those with needs. Those who embrace Socialism may be impressed by its ideals, but its real world economic performance is dismal. The Socialistic system requires governmental <u>compulsion</u> whereas Free Enterprise is consensual. Cuba and North Korea are dictatorships. Under Socialism people are not free.

These two economic systems are dividing America. The America that works and contributes, and the America that doesn't. Socialism has reduced Detroit to a bankrupt city. Do we want the same kind of dysfunctional government on a national basis? That is where we are headed. Is working hard and smart to become wealthy a sin? Churchill said it best, "In an economic system where some people cannot become rich, everyone will be poor."

What makes Free Enterprise so successful? In Free Enterprise there is a need to make a **"profit"** and earn a **"return on the investment."** These financial concepts build wealth, bur are misunderstood, or treated as greed.

Here is the Wharton School of Business definition of profit.

*"Profit is the earned reward for efficiently supplying a social good."*

Businesses compete in very aggressive antagonistic markets. To survive, every business must supply a quality product or service at appealing prices while controlling the cost of doing business so that a profit is earned. That is why profit is an "earned reward," and it is difficult to earn.

The opposite of profit is "loss." Taking a loss means that the net worth of the business has declined. If the losses continue the business will run out of cash and close its doors. Would you want to work for a company that was losing money and running a deficit? Profit provides job security and the money for growth. The wealth of the United States is created by millions of profitable businesses in the private sector, not by government. Government does not produce wealth, it taxes and redistributes it.

There is another important reason for a business to make a profit. Money has been put at risk when it is *invested* in the business. The hope is that the business will succeed and earn money. It is not different from earning interest on a savings account or a CD at the bank. Earnings on all investments are called returns. For private citizens it is called savings. Since business is very risky, the profit is called the return. When comparing the return to the money invested, it should be sufficient to justify the risks taken when making the investment.

Every year thousands of businesses, both new and old, go broke. The mortality rate on new businesses is not pretty: 24% fail within two years; 51% close within 4 years; and 63% shut down within 6 years. The rate of return must cover the risks, or the business will fail.

It takes skilled managers who run successful businesses? They are called <u>entrepreneurs.</u> Entrepreneurs take the risks to start and manage businesses. Entrepreneurs are always looking for creative new ways to "make money." They "visualize" a future improvement that requires taking risks to bring that creative concept to reality. If the idea makes life better for people they will freely exchange their hard-earned money for products or services that enhance their lives. And those who supply those benefits have earned the right to receive a fair profit if they run their businesses efficiently and competitively.

Bill Gates, the founder of Microsoft, provided better software. It has helped to ease work, improve productivity, and provide pleasure for hundred of millions of people. Steve Jobs changed the fundamental nature of communication. Bill and Steve earned their wealth.

Surprisingly, the wealthier people are, the more charitable they are. Bill Gates and Warren Buffett are good examples. This is the pattern of most wealthy people. There is only so much they can spend on themselves, and they fear spoiling their children. They give huge portions of their income and wealth to philanthropic endeavors and charities. Wealthy people generally are honest, humble, and charitable.

Yet some Americans believe most business executives are greedy and dishonest. Dishonest greed is indeed bad; its goal is to use fraud and theft to take from others without an honest exchange. The few dishonest businessmen get a disproportionate amount of publicity while the vast majority of honest managers are taken for granted.

It has been my experience that most business executives have excellent ethics, and it is not an accident. **Honesty is a necessity for success**. Success in business requires keeping customers happy. If customers are treated dishonestly they don't come back and they tell others. Soon the business has a bad reputation and fails. A business can grow only by providing an honest product or service over many years. The good reputation spreads by "word of mouth" and the business prospers.

*The American Dream is that anybody can become wealthy!* Why not? The desire for a better life is a fundamental survival instinct of all human beings. Our Founding Fathers created the Free Enterprise System in our Constitution - a precious gift that has made the United States one of the wealthiest of nations.

## INGREDIENTS OF THE FREE ENTERPRISE SYSTEM

1. THE RIGHT OF OWNERSHIP guaranteed by the government. That is what Capitalism is all about, the *right of ownership* to keep the wealth you create. If you want to own a car, a home, or a business -- then you are a Capitalist.
2. FREE MARKETS where competition between several buyers and sellers permits deals to be made by "mutual consent," not coercion.
3. A STABLE GOVERNMENT RESPONSIVE TO THE PEOPLE where at least two political parties compete in honest regular secret elections to select candidates whose power is limited, and who work hard and honestly to serve the citizens.
4. STABLE MONEY where the long-term value of the currency is dependable.
5. RULE OF LAW, WHERE CONTRACTS MAY BE ENFORCED WITH HONEST COURTS THAT RULE

WITH PREDICTABLE CONSISTENCY. This assures that contracts can be legally enforced without prejudice.

6. REASONABLE TAX LEVELS THAT DO NOT DESTROY THE INCENTIVE TO MAKE INVESTMENTS. Throughout history, when the combination of taxes approach 50%, entrepreneurs refrain from starting, expanding, or creating new jobs that generate higher standards of living.

7. A WIDESPREAD UNDERSTANDING OF THE DOUBLE ENTRY ACCOUNTING SYSTEM is necessary because without that knowledge, people cannot determine if a business is making a profit or going bankrupt.

8. A POPULAR ATTITUDE EMBRACING THE IDEA THAT ANYONE CAN BECOME WEALTHY (THE AMERICAN DREAM).

As the above ingredients are removed from a nation's economy, growth declines and poverty increases. Few of these ingredients are available in North Korea and the people are starving. With Free Enterprise, entrepreneurs become rich, the middle class grows and prospers, the least skilled have jobs, and the lazy few still live in poverty and need charity.

When government, be it a city, state, or national grows more slowly than their private sector, there is prosperity, the opposite is Socialism.

## WHY DOES SOCIALISM FAIL?

Governments do not have a profit motive or need for a return on investment. They operate for political popularity so elected officials can stay in office. Milton and Rose Friedman wrote a book, *Free to Choose*. It won the Nobel Prize in Economics describing the attitudes when people spend money. It helps us understand why government is so naturally wasteful. Let's review the four ways people spend money.

1. Spend your money on yourself.
2. Spend your money on other people.
3. Spend other people's money on your self.
4. Spend other people's money on other people (government).

It's just common sense. When we spend our own hard-earned money on ourselves, we are most careful. We are still careful when spending our money on a loved one or friend. We become less careful when we spend someone else's money on ourselves. Care nearly vanishes when we spend other peoples' money on other people.

That's what governments do; spend other people's money on other people. And that is why governments are naturally disorganized, inefficient, and too often corrupt. It makes no difference if it is a city, state, or nation, size does not change human nature. Larger government just means bigger inefficiency and waste. With the Federal Reserve buying bonds to finance

U.S. deficits, it is easy to understand why Washington has no discipline or thrift. Wasteful spending is out of control.

Reliable research has proven that large government and large government debt actually reduce the growth of a nation's economy. The total value of a nations annual production is called the Gross Domestic Product (GDP). It is a reasonably accurate measure of the value of a nation's annual productive wealth.

Research done for the Joint Economic Committee of Congress by Professors James Gwartney, Robert Lawson, and Randall Holcombe showed that **as government grows larger as a percent of GDP the nation's growth slows**. This study has been repeatedly confirmed as correct and it makes sense. Because the private sector is more efficient than the government, the larger government is as a share of the total GDP of a nation, the less prosperity citizens will enjoy. Here are the numbers from that study.

## DEVELOPED COUNTRIES 1960-1996

| Size of Government as % GDP | GDP Growth |
|---|---|
| Less than 25% | 6.6% |
| 25-29% | 4.7% |
| 30-39% | 3.8% |
| 40-49% | 2.8% |
| 50-59% | 2.0% |
| Over 60% | 1.6% or less |

As you can see, this study was made a few decades ago when the industrialized nations had much less debt than today. If these studies were repeated today, the growth numbers would be much smaller. We know this is true because new frightening research has discovered that the higher government debt is as a percent of GDP, the debt is a drag on growth. Government spending does stimulate economic growth when <u>debt levels are low</u>, but <u>fails to stimulate new growth when debt ratios are high. This is further aggravated when the nation is running a high budget deficit as a percent of GDP</u>.

The problem is that of solvency, the ability of the nation to pay its bills. These numbers from 2010 show that most of the large nations on our planet are technically bankrupt.

| COUNTRY | DEBT/GDP | DEFICIT |
|---------|----------|---------|
| Japan | 200% | 10% |
| Italy | 115% | 10% |
| Greece | 113% | 9% |
| Belgium | 99% | 8% |
| Iceland | 95% | 7% |
| <u>USA</u> | <u>100%</u> | <u>9%</u> |
| Spain | 90% | 8% |
| France | 80% | 8% |
| Germany | 77% | 4% |
| Portugal | 75% | 11% |
| England | 69% | 10% |
| Ireland | 64% | 14% |
| China | 18% | ? |

The research justifies the concern that many Americans have about the size of our national debt. Research has proven that that when the ratio of government debt exceeds 70% of GDP private sector growth slows. When the debt ratio reaches 90% of GDP, government deficit spending fails to stimulate new growth. As the debt to GDP continues higher, the drag on growth accelerates. U.S. debt is acknowledged to be in excess of $18 trillion. Our annual GDP is just over $16 trillion, so our debt ratio is over 100%! Some calculations place it much higher.

If you have doubts about how oppressive high government debt is to growth, here is proof. These numbers appeared in the Monday, August 6, 2012 issue of the *Wall Street Journal* and show how increased government spending failed to reverse the decline in GDP. Deficit financed spending didn't deliver growth.

| COUNTRY | Change in Government Spending as a Percent of GDP from 2007 to 2009. | Change in Real GDP Growth from 2006-07 to 2008-09. |
| --- | --- | --- |
| United States | +7.3% | -8.4% |
| Japan | +6.7% | -10.5% |
| Germany | +4.6% | -11.6% |
| France | +4.1% | -7.7% |
| United Kingdom | +6.9% | -11.5% |
| Italy | +4.3% | -10.5% |
| Canada | +4.9% | -7.1% |
| Australia | +3.3% | -3.5% |
| Spain | +6.9% | -10.4% |
| Mexico | +5.2% | -13.5% |
| Korea | +1.1% | -7.7% |
| Turkey | +4.4% | -15.7% |
| Netherlands | +5.7% | -9.0% |
| Sweden | +3.8% | -13.6% |
| Poland | +2.3% | -6.3% |
| Norway | +6.2% | -6.7% |
| Belgium | +5.5% | -7.5% |
| Austria | +4.3% | -9.8% |
| Denmark | +7.1% | -11.6% |
| Chile | +5.2% | -8.9% |
| Greece | +6.3% | -11.0% |
| Finland | +8.7% | -17.8% |
| Portugal | +5.5% | -6.7% |
| Ireland | +11.7% | -20.5% |
| Czech Republic | +3.9% | -14.4% |
| New Zealand | +3.4% | -6.0% |
| Hungary | +0.7% | -9.9% |
| Slovak Republic | +7.5% | -18.0% |
| Luxembourg | +6.8% | -16.2% |
| Slovenia | +6.1% | -17.1% |
| Estonia | 12.8% | -35.5% |
| Iceland | +7.4% | -16.2% |

The most frightening problems developed nations face is the rising cost of their *future unfunded obligations*. This future burden is transitioning our economy more and more toward socialism with very unpleasant financial consequences.

The demographics of the ageing populations in western nations projects that there are too few young people to pay into these programs to sustain the benefit systems. They are actuarially beyond the taxing and borrowing capability of most nations. According to *Investors Business Daily*, "In Greece 100 grandparents have 42 grandchildren; the family tree is upside down. If 100 geezers run up a bazillion dollars worth of debt, will 42 youngsters ever be able to pay it off?"

According to the Chase Bank, U.S. combined unfunded liabilities are somewhere between $70 and $100 trillion. That's not billions, its trillions. Our unfunded debt is probably six times our GDP! Without financial discipline, another very serious financial crisis is ahead.

Like it or not, the budgets of Western industrialized nations cannot be balanced without reform of the retirement, medical care, and other benefit programs. Politicians know this must be done but fear defeat in the next election. Without reform, the outcome will be either **rapid inflation**, government **default,** or **both**.

History has shown that rapid inflation is the most destructive morally, politically and financially to a people. Hyperinflation happened in the Weimar Republic in Germany. In 1921 inflation was only 6%. A year later in 1922, inflation jumped to 200%. In 1923 the money became worthless and unacceptable in trade. It took a wheelbarrow of money to buy a loaf of bread. Inflation accelerated so fast that the empty bottle of wine, drunk for dinner the night before, was worth more than the full bottle the previous evening. German hyperinflation produced loose morals, a terrible depression, anarchy, and lead to the election of a dictator, Adolph Hitler. We Americans once went own that path.

Our first government, the Continental Congress also issued money that became worthless in just three years. Do we want to repeat that error? If the Federal Reserve increases our money supply to finance our deficits, it will eventually cause inflation. Inflation is a hidden tax! The following chart shows the actual destruction of buying power of the U.S. dollar during the last century from 1900 to 2000. The decline was **slow**, so people hardly noticed it, but over 100 years it destroyed over 97% of the value of the dollar.

Rapid inflation is a catastrophe. It destroys savings, makes bonds worthless, punishes moral behavior, pauperizes savers, and eventually the money in no longer acceptable in trade. Business comes to a near halt, unemployment rises, there are riots in the streets, and that sets the stage for a dictator. Hyperinflation is the worst of worst outcomes.

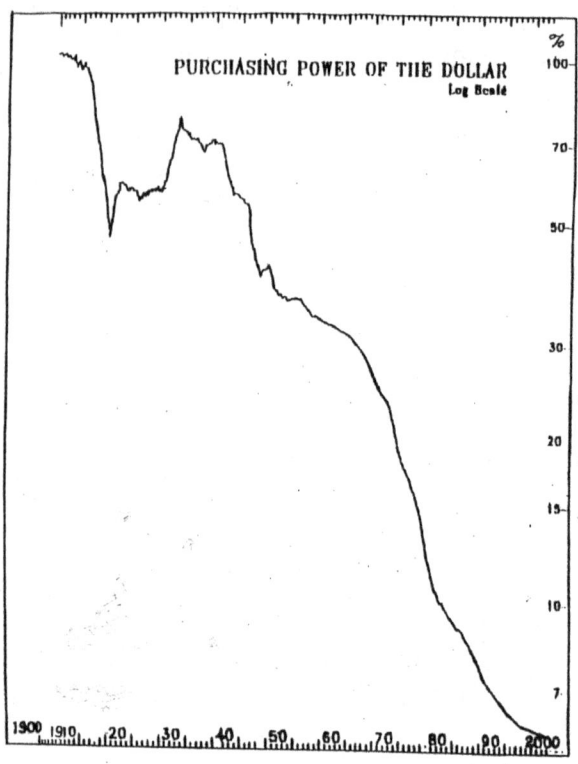

PURCHASING POWER OF THE DOLLAR
Log Scale

The second way governments go bankrupt is called **"default'**. One night the Soviet Union went broke and the next morning it ceased to exist. It simply ran out of money and closed down. The ruble lost over 95% of its value overnight. When a country defaults, its debt obligations and currency become worthless. Soviet employees, the military, and all citizens dependant on government for social benefits didn't get paid. All USSR financial obligations become worthless. Years of financial turmoil followed.

There are a number of warning signals leading to default and unfortunately the US economy seems to be going down that road. First the credit rating agencies lower the credit rating on the government's debt. U.S. DEBT has been reduced from AAA to AA. Lower credit ratings force governments to pay higher interest rates in order to borrow money. Higher rates increase the cost of debt payments further increasing the deficit and building more debt. A debt spiral ends in default where the government ceases to meet its obligations.

Can we allow this to happen in the United States? No other nation is big enough to bail us out so we would take the world down with us. Do we want global financial chaos and a worldwide depression? If not, we need to get our government spending under control.

Will our politicians prevent inflation or default? Will they act in time?

I learned a valuable lesson from President Gerald Ford in the Oval Office. In the late 1970's, my research convinced me that because of risky lending on over-valued real estate, the Savings and Loan industry in the U.S. was headed for a financial crisis. I prepared a proposal that suggested a way to prevent the crisis and shared it with the chairman of a local bank. It excited him so much that he made arrangements for us to present it to President Ford at the White House.

President Ford explained why even if the strategy could work, it was not *politically* feasible. He said that businessmen try to anticipate problems and prevent them from occurring in order to enhance profits, but that doesn't work in government. If the public is *not aware* that there is a potential problem, and successful action is taken to prevent it, there is *no political upside*. But, if while trying to solve a problem that the public does not know about *something goes wrong*, there is *serious political downside*.

He explained that governments wait till the public demands action on a problem before doing "something." If the public has the *"perception"* that the government action is good, then politically things are okay even if the action taken is ineffective. President Ford was totally truthful emphasizing that political "perception" was everything. I believe him.

Here is a frightening example of what socialistic dictatorships do. Communism does not permit the right of private ownership of property. Before the Communist revolution Russia was the "Breadbasket of Europe." For generations large farms owned by experienced farmers called Kulaks produced Russia's agricultural wealth. Their export of grains and vegetables throughout Europe was the source of the Tsar's treasure.

The Soviet Union told these Kulaks that the state now owned their farms. The Kulaks objected, so *they were executed*. With the death of the Kulaks the Russian people lost the precious management skills and knowledge to produce crops successfully and profitably. Communes of peasants were formed to run the farms, but they didn't know how to do it successfully. The following year the Soviet Union barely had enough food to feed its own people, and thereafter there <u>never</u>

<u>ever again was enough food</u>. When the Union of Soviet Socialistic Republics failed, millions of its people were starving.

Ayn Rand, the famous Russian author, asks, "By what right do those who can work and don't, make demands on those who do work for a share of their hard-earned money?" Perhaps that sounds too harsh, but independence and self-reliance are what grows people into their best selves.

Years of prosperity followed after Margaret Thatcher privatized England's public housing by selling them to their occupants as condos. She also privatized the railroads, stood up to the excessive union demands, and shrank the government bureaucracy. England prospered and their economy soon passed Socialistic France. Smaller government works.

We need to do the same with our government, and only a Constitutional Convention can make it happen.

Now let me show you visible proof of the dynamics of the Free Enterprise System and the failure of Socialism. Here are two nighttime satellite photographs taken 300 miles above the earth. The first shows North and South Korea. Freedom and the Free Enterprise System are visible from the lights seen in South Korea. In the Socialistic North even their capital city is in darkness.

The next page has another satellite night view of our wonderful United States. It shows the bright lights of Free Enterprise and a Free People. With two-term limits and citizen patriots in Congress, there will be enough courage to reverse the trend to socialism and restore Free Enterprise. Let's keep the American dream alive by calling a Constitutional Convention! It's the only way.

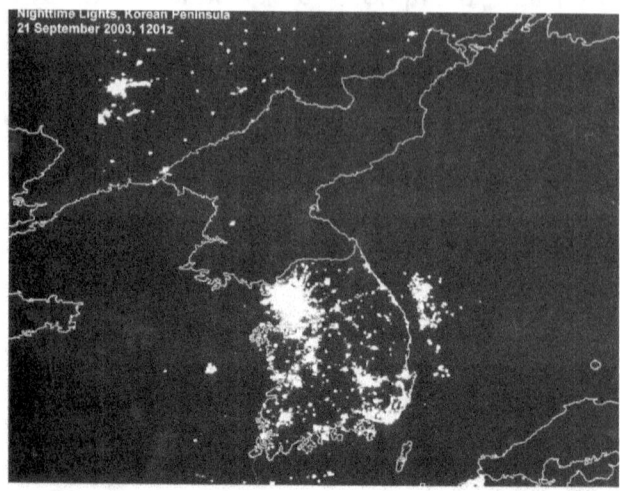

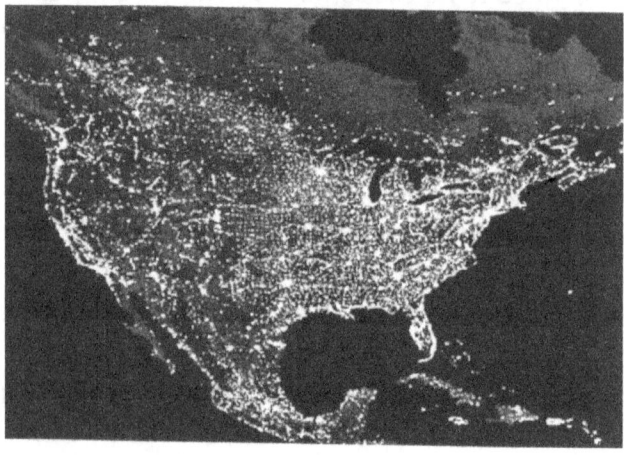

# CONCLUSION

*"We hold these Truths to be self-evident, that all Men are created equal, that they are endowed by their Creator with certain unalienable Rights, that among these are Life, Liberty, and the pursuit of Happiness –"*

The Declaration of Independence defining Freedom

We Americans are optimists, hard working, creative, honest, people who love our country. Our industries lead the world as beacons of innovation and productivity.

Our Founding Fathers sacrificed their lives and fortunes as a sacred duty. They founded this great nation and blessed us with a remarkable Constitution. But they could not anticipate the breakthroughs in science, technology, medicine or the explosion in communications like phones, television, and the Internet. We know Washington is dysfunctional. Will be do nothing or will we carry the Torch of Liberty forward? Our Constitution is hurting will we heal it? Shall we responsibly continue the work of our Founding Fathers?

Term limits, election reform, and ethical standards for our public servants would be awesome improvements for our society and posterity. Additional Amendments could modernize and complete the healing of our Constitution. We can restore our nation and herald in a bright new future. States revise their constitutions, and cities revise their charters every few decades. Our Constitution is overdue for love and care. Modernizing our Constitution can restore and protect our freedoms, explode opportunities, and assure prosperity for us, and future generations.

Since these needed changes will not come from Washington, only a Constitutional Convention can make this happen. The assembly of such an important body of patriotic men and women would be a triumphant historical achievement. Our Founding Fathers are watching to see if we are inspired to lead a rebirth of freedom. Shall we act?

Writing officials in Washington is useless. Write, email, and phone the political leaders of your state. Google their addresses on the Internet. Please tell them we urgently need legislation calling a Constitutional Convention. The last pages of this book have that suggested legislation. Photocopy it and send it with your letter. Insist on quick action.

Urge your family, friends, and everyone you know to do the same. State governments will respond if enough people demand a Constitutional Convention. We the People must speak. We can no longer remain silent, and we must not fail!

*Choose Life, Liberty and the Pursuit of Happiness!*

## HELP MAKE IT HAPPEN!

## RESOLUTIONS FROM 34 STATES ARE NECESSARY

### THE REPAIR WASHINGTON RESOLUTION
### A CONTINUING RESOLUTION TO CALL A CONVENTION TO SUCCESSFULLY AMEND THE CONSTITUTION

**BY:** *(sponsors for Louisiana's Legislature in April 2015)*

**U.S. CONSTITUTION:** *Applies and orders the U.S. Congress to promptly convene a Constitutional Convention on a specific date, leaving all other decisions and powers to the state legislatures and their appointed delegates as to the location, qualifications for delegates, procedures, and finances as provided for herein. The Constitutional Convention shall propose amendments for ratification by the states as part of the Constitution. Delegates are prohibited and instructed to oppose amendments that alter the Bill of Rights, limit civil rights, reduce personal freedoms, or create special privileges. Amendments shall address term limits, election procedures and reform, ethics for public servants, financial discipline, a Countermand Amendment, and other appropriate matters to modernize the Constitution and enhance the freedoms, opportunities, and prosperity of the people.*

**WHEREAS** *political power is vested with the People, and*

**WHEREAS** *the People have consented to self-government by granting limited powers to the States, and*

**WHEREAS** *the States ordered the original Constitutional Convention, and*

**WHEREAS** *the States ratified the proposed Constitution thus creating a central government called the United States of America and granting to it limited powers, and*

**WHEREAS** *Article V of that Constitution as well as the powers granted to the States by the People permit the calling of another Constitutional Convention, and*

**WHEREAS** *most cities update their charters every few decades, and States update their Constitutions about every 100 years, and the United States Constitution has not been updated for over 235 years, and*

**WHEREAS** *the calling of a Constitutional Convention is legal, long overdue and urgently needed,*

**THEREFORE BE IT RESOLVED** *that the Legislature of Louisiana does hereby apply to and order the United States Congress to promptly, within thirty days of the two-thirds (34) of the state legislatures having passed this or similar resolutions, promptly set the date for the convening of a Constitutional Convention, such date being no sooner than five months or later than six months from the date of that two-thirds event, and further that Congress, the President and Supreme Court have no powers or authority other than to set that date;*

*and should the Congress fail to promptly comply, the States and/or their delegations are authorized to act independently, as is their right, to take such action as necessary to convene the Convention.*

**BE IT FURTHER RESOLVED** *that Delegates are prohibited and are instructed to oppose amendments that alter the Bill of Rights, limit civil rights, reduce any freedoms of the People, or in any way create special privileges.*

**BE IT FURTHER RESOLVED THAT THE OBJECTIVES OF THE CONVENTION ARE** *to recommend Amendments to the United States Constitution that shall, if ratified, make our national government more responsive to the long-term best interests and freedoms of all citizens by addressing term limits, election procedures and reform, ethics for public servants, financial discipline, a Countermand Amendment, and other appropriate changes to the United States Government that will modernize the Constitution and expand the opportunities and prosperity of the people. The Convention rules of order will seek to emulate the conditions present at the First Constitutional Convention by providing security, privacy, and procedures for open discussion that encourage neither haste nor delay, wise decisions, and recommendations of acceptable amendments.*

## BE IT FURTHER RESOLVED

**STATE DELEGATIONS AND DELEGATES.** *Each state may send a Delegation to the Convention. Each*

Delegation shall have one vote, equal rights, privileges, authority, and all else necessary to accomplish the Convention's Objectives. Each state may, in any manner it sees fit, elect or appoint no less than three and no more than seven Official Delegates to represent their state's interests at the convention. Two Alternate Delegates may be elected to substitute for any Official Delegates unable to serve for any reason.

**QUALIFICATIONS FOR OFFICIAL DELEGATES AND ALTERNATES.** Delegates and alternates must be United States citizens, no less than 40 years of age, and with a reputation for honesty, hard work, intelligence, and patriotism. No person shall be eligible to serve as a Delegate if he or she is serving or has been in the Federal Government in any elected, judicial, appointed or employed position; nor has ever been convicted as a felon, declared bankruptcy, or been employed as a lobbyist. The Convention may select non-voting advisors that may include past Presidents of the United States and active members of our Armed Forces, subject to the same qualifications as Official Delegates.

**ORGANIZATION.** After no less than 20 Delegations have been empowered by their state, a temporary convening committee shall be appointed from those states to determine where, and if necessary when (should Congress fail to promptly do so), the Convention shall convene, certify the qualifications of all Delegates, provide credentials, and make all necessary arrangements to convene the Convention.

*Upon convening, the Convention shall elect the Administrative Committee charged with the full responsibility for the operation and rules of order for the Convention. The Administrative Committee is further empowered to discharge any Delegate for cause, or breach of secrecy or security, or conflict of interest; however a majority vote of the Convention may at any time overrule a decision of the Administrative Committee, and change any of its members*

*At no time will any Delegation be denied its right and responsibility to represent its state by voting on every motion and amendment. Any absence of one or more Official Delegates from a Delegation shall not deny that Delegation its right to vote. Should the Administrative Committee disqualify any Official Delegate, the next Alternate Delegate from that state shall immediately fill their place with full authority.*

**FINANCE.** *The cost for the operation of the Constitutional Convention shall be borne equally among all states. To cover Convention operations, every state shall promptly send no less than two million dollars to officially install their Delegation. Additional requests for funds shall be borne equally among all the states and shall be paid promptly, or their Delegation may not vote.*

*Within forty-five days after the Convention is adjourned, all financial obligations are to be promptly settled with a full accounting of all costs presented to every state, and all remaining funds equally distributed among the states.*

*Each state shall bear all of the personal and living expenses of its Official and Alternate Delegates.*

**PRIVACY and SECURITY.** *The Convention shall appoint a Security Committee charged with the responsibility and authority to maintain privacy, secrecy, and assure that all Convention activities, meetings, communications, documents and conversations shall be confidential. It will foster conditions for thoughtful and respectful communications between Official Delegates, and working conditions conducive to the origination of prudent, practical, and politically acceptable Amendments for ratification.*

*The committee shall prohibit members of the press, lobbyists, and any unauthorized persons from coming in or near the venue, subject to arrest for trespassing, fine of $100,000, and imprisonment for no less than one year at the cost of and with the cooperation of the state in which the Convention is held.*

*The committee shall have full authority to select and employ reliable security forces sufficient to provide the necessary safety, secrecy and security of all Delegates.*

**PATRIOTISM.** *All Official Delegates to the Convention shall take the following oath. "I swear to faithfully serve the American People by fulfilling my duties as a Delegate to this Convention. I promise to respect and cooperate with other Delegates, work with patriotism, and recommend amendments for the betterment of the nation, so help me God."*

*Delegations shall work with reasonable expedition presenting Amendments to the states for ratification only after all of the work is complete, said Amendments having been approved by a majority of the Delegations at adjournment of the Convention.*

**BE IT FURTHER RESOLVED** *that the Louisiana secretary of state is hereby directed to transmit copies of this resolution to the president and secretary of the United States Senate and the speaker and clerk of the United States House of Representatives, and copies hereof to the presiding officers of each of the legislative houses of the several states, requesting their cooperation.*

**BE IT FURTHER RESOLVED** *that this resolution constitutes a continuing application in accordance with Article V of the Constitution of the United States until the legislatures of at least two-thirds of the several states have passed such resolutions.*

# SIDNEY PULITZER

Gilmore in support of submarines. In 1949 Pulitzer joined Wemco (formerly Wembley, Inc.), the world's largest men's neckwear manufacturer. He was elected president in 1976, chairman and chief executive officer in 1989, and chairman in 1995. Wemco employed over 750 personnel, selling over sixty million dollars of neckwear and sports apparel worldwide. The firm was sold in 1997. Pulitzer also served as president and chairman of the National Neckwear Association and in 1987 received its Achievement Award as Manufacturer of the Year.

A native of New Orleans, Sidney C. Pulitzer is a graduate of the Wharton School of Finance at the University of Pennsylvania, with a Bachelor of Science in Economics.

He served two years as an officer in the US Navy aboard the USS Howard

Prior to publishing "Repair Washington" Pulitzer authored three books on banking and one on military preparedness. In 1968, he incorporated Advance Planning Inc, a SEC-registered investment firm providing Investment Counseling services now available on the Internet at Ltgrowth.com.

He has served in many civic and charitable organizations including president and chairman of the World Trade Center of New Orleans, past Division Chairman of the United Way of Greater New Orleans, Chairman of Young Presidents Organization of Louisiana, board member of Touro Infirmary, Newman School, Touro Synagogue, Willow Wood Home of the Aged, and Country Day School.

Sidney Pulitzer is in his 20th year as Adjunct Professor of Entrepreneurship in the Freeman School of Business at Tulane University. He twice received the Wisner Award for outstanding teaching, and the Tulane Entrepreneur of the Year Award for 2011.

He is married to the former Joyce Samuelson, and they develop and manage commercial and residential real estate. They have a son, Sidney Copeland Pulitzer, Jr., daughter, C.C. Lemann, and two grandsons, Monte Lemann III, and Spencer Lemann.
EMAIL: scpulitzer@yahoo.com